Empowered Empath

NAVIGATING THE SEVEN STAGES OF AN EMPATH AWAKENING & UNDERSTANDING WHAT IT TRULY MEANS TO BE AN EMPATH

EMPOWERED EMPATH SERIES
BOOK ONE

JENNIFER O'NEILL

Empowered Empath: *Navigating the Seven Stages of An Empath Awakening & Understanding What it Truly Means to Be An Empath*

Copyright © 2024 by Jennifer O'Neill

All Rights Reserved.

No part of this publication may be reproduced, distributed, or transmitted in any form or by any means, including photocopying, recordings, or other electronic or mechanical methods, without the prior written permission of the publisher, except in the case of brief quotations embodied in reviews and certain other noncommercial uses permitted by copyright law.

Disclaimer: This book is designed to provide accurate and authoritative information in regard to the subject matter covered. By its sale, neither the publisher nor the author of this book does not dispense medical advice or prescribe the use of any technique as a form of treatment for physical, emotional, or medical problems without the advice of a physician, either directly or indirectly. The intent of the author is only to offer information of a general nature to help you in your quest for spiritual well-being. In the event you use any of the information in this book for yourself, the author and the publisher assume no responsibility for your actions.

Keys to the Spirit World, LLC

Kailua, HI 96734

www.keystothespiritworld.com

First Kindle Edition: September 2024

ISBN: 978-1-64034-678-9

Contents

Introduction	v
Part I	1
1. The Struggling Empath	3
2. The Energetic Eco System	9
3. Common Misconception & Hurdles	15
4. Understanding Your Empath Ability	20
5. Why You Were Chosen	23
6. Being an Empath vs Empathy: What's the Difference?	29
7. Empath Traits & Characteristics	35
8. What Kind of Empath Are You?	49
9. Five Types of Empath Energies	53
10. Twelve Types of Empaths & Empath Labeling	58
11. Resistance & Acceptance	69
12. Living An Empowered Empath Lifestyle	79
13. What Happens During an Empath Awakening	83
Part II	89
14. Stage 1 – Spiritual Crisis	91
15. Stage 2 – Spiritual Depression	98
16. Stage 3 – Spiritual Purpose	112
17. Stage 4 – Spiritual Awareness	121
18. Stage 5 - Spiritual Sponge	132
19. Stage 6 – Spiritual Release	145
20. Stage 7 – Spiritual Clearing & Development	153
21. Bridging the Gap	164
Quantum Heart Meditation	167
About the Author	169

Introduction

When it comes to being an Empath or understanding an Empath's ability, there's a lot of information out there. While some of the information is valid, there is a huge component "missing." When you have a subject as complex as this one, where some of the most important information you need is missing, it makes the entire landscape a lot harder to navigate.

For instance, if someone gives you a map for the purpose of navigating a specific area, and some of the roads or landmarks are missing, you are quickly going to realize it's a lot harder to navigate than if you'd been given all the information in the first place. This means you will have to take the time to fill in the blank spots, which can also leave you feeling unsure of yourself and second-guessing things. And even if you do things properly, filling in all the blanks can take years...

Why is this information missing?

I don't believe these things have been left out purposely. I believe the information being delivered is derived from their place of knowledge, which is typically a space occupied by those who are well versed with the physical body, the physical world, and physical experiences.

INTRODUCTION

This creates a huge problem for those of you who are interested in learning more about **what it really means to be an Empath**, because you will *never, ever* be able to fully understand how this ability works or how it fits into your life without a complete understanding of how the ENTIRE process works.

Can you still work with an Empath ability and navigate through life without understanding how the entire process works? Or more importantly WHY it works?

Of course! Will you be able to feel the healthiest or feel good while doing it? Not likely. But here's the interesting thing—there is a large portion of the population currently walking around with an Empath ability, *yet they have no idea they have it.* Let alone how many issues it's causing them and how it might be affecting their health and wellness. This is definitely a problem!

That same part of the population is struggling with anything from light to chronic health issues, depression, and anxiety. But they are focusing in the wrong place—their physical body and western medicine, which seems reasonable, because they feel as if their body is failing them somehow. This is what we've been taught. We've been trained to understand things from a very physical perspective. How to be physical and live a very physical lifestyle. Live physical, think physical, breathe physical, and see physical.

But what if these health issues do not stem from the physical body?

What if their body is not failing them at all? What if something else is going on? What if they have an ability that works with another aspect of who they are? Something that feels very physical but it's not. It feels the same but works differently...

I have taken this journey myself, and what I've discovered has led me to an awareness that's been life changing.

However, this book is NOT for everyone!

INTRODUCTION

Before you read this book:

1) You must have an open mind.

2) You must be willing to challenge your beliefs and how you *think* the physical world currently works around you.

3) You must be okay with *being different and thinking differently* than those around you and not to worry that they will adapt to your new perspective.

This book is for you, your health, and your alignment, and nobody else. Their mindset doesn't matter, their perspective doesn't matter, their journey doesn't matter...

So who's it for?

1) It's for those who may **know or wonder** if they are an Empath.

2) It's for those who've **been struggling** with health issues, depression, or anxiety.

3) It's for those who **don't feel well** and find themselves frustrated because they're being told, *You're fine, there's nothing wrong with you.*

4) It's for those who are **mentally exhausted** looking for answers on how to live a more organic, clean, and spiritually connected way of living. One based upon power and not weakness.

5) For those who want to *feel stronger*, who want to *feel more connected*, who want to *feel smarter* because they

INTRODUCTION

understand the map of knowledge that they've been given is missing something...something important, but they just can't put their finger on what it is.

I'm going to give you knowledge, I'm going to challenge your beliefs, and I'm going to help you to understand why this moment in time right now is a blessing.

But it's not going to be easy. You're not only going to learn about this gift, but you're going to be asked to let go of some things.

And letting go is not easy.

You will have to let go of many things. Old beliefs, old habits, old patterns. Your current way of doing things will become your old way of doing things.

But if you consume this knowledge with an open mind and take the time to utilize this knowledge by adhering to a new way of life, a way of finding balance—balance between the physical and spiritual worlds...

If you are willing to integrate it into your everyday life, you will embark on the most rewarding journey of your life...

Part One

**Section 1
What It Means to Be an Empath**

CHAPTER 1
The Struggling Empath

For years I tried many, many things to help me understand what was happening. For years I felt horrible, and all I wanted was to *feel better*.

The interesting thing is I had no idea it had anything to do with my spiritual senses or this powerful gift I was born with. All I knew was time after time I was experiencing things that made my body feel weak, I felt sick, and this made me feel worried and fearful all the time. I spent many, many years and hours of my life going to the doctor. Checking one thing, then another. Constantly being told I was fine, everything looked good. I felt let down. I felt let down by the doctors, I felt let down by my body, and I didn't know what to do.

Just because they didn't find anything didn't mean I didn't feel good. I didn't feel well at all. I started thinking, *Am I just nuts? Could this all be in my head?* I could tell everyone around me was wondering this too, which made me feel even worse, ashamed even. I didn't want people to see me that way —heck, I didn't want to see myself that way! But I did...and that didn't feel good either.

However, something wasn't sitting right. I couldn't put my finger on it, but something was missing. Deep down I knew I wasn't exaggerating what was going on. It was how I felt.

Slowly but surely, I started putting together what *it* was. Over time, the more I worked professionally in the world of healing, I started noticing patterns. Not only in my life, but with clients as well. And this is where things started taking a turn for the better. These patterns gave me a direction, a place to explore, and I was very curious... *What was going on here?*

When I knew where to look, it became apparent what I had been struggling with for so many years was tied to my spiritual senses. I thought, *Awesome!* I know how to navigate this area; in fact, I'm very skilled at it. It's what I do! But that's when the next letdown came...

I learned that it wasn't just a spiritual gift, like all my other gifts, but it was different and way more complex. And to be truthful, the complexity was a little mindboggling. It wasn't just a skill that I could learn to understand, develop, and use at will like I had with my other abilities. My other abilities were way more controllable. Typically, when you are working with your spiritual senses there are techniques you can use so you are not "on" all the time in a way that affects your physical health. Especially if you are trained in this area.

But the same rules didn't apply here. This ability was very different; there was no on/off switch. In fact, it did not work at all like my other spiritual senses (seeing, touching, hearing, knowing), but it seemed to be part of who I was on a soul level. It integrated and intertwined with my spiritual and physical bodies in a way that I had not been aware of before. Which meant several things:

- It was harder to control and manage.

- It was part of my day-to-day life whether I wanted it to be or not.

Being an Empath is different, very different. Unlike other spiritual gifts, this one is overpowering, overwhelming, and will push its way into every nook and cranny of your life…

But I was on a mission. I was going to do as much research as I could. I was determined to learn how to train this ability and make it manageable. And this brought me to my next letdown.

I discovered that everything I was being taught through books or other psychics was either incorrect information or that they had left out a gigantic portion of information. What I discovered was most of the things people teach about being an Empath focuses upon such a small portion that the knowledge is not very effective.

It's like being taught about one country, when you really need to have information about the whole world in your knowledge base. Let me tell you, that doesn't work very well. Nothing made sense. I knew there was so much information that was missing, and this information wasn't out there… which meant I was left to explore this whole vast area and learn things by myself.

I wanted to know more… What does it mean? Being an Empath? Exactly what does it mean? (And this is where my first pet peeve lies, because there's a lot of cookie-cutter information out there, some of which I'm sure you've already heard.)

The dictionary version refers to a form of extrasensory perception where a person acquires psychic knowledge primarily by means of empathic feelings and emotions.

Which means you can *feel* what's going on with another person **emotionally**.

While this is accurate information to a degree, it's about five or ten percent of what being an Empath actually means, and it's a very small portion of your Empathic gift.

Where I think this causes a problem is it allows people, or trains people, to focus on this area specifically. Which means you primarily focus upon other people's emotions. *"Oh, I'm feeling all these feelings from everybody else and all these emotions. I need to be able to manage this!"*

What's not apparent in this flawed premise is there's quite a bit more you need to know when it comes to managing this ability.

Understanding your Empath ability means understanding there is so much more to it than being able to *feel people* and the ability to *feel their emotions*.

What being an Empath actually means is possessing the ability to read energy…ALL ENERGY.

That makes this ability so much more powerful than all the other psychic senses because there's so much more energy flowing through the Earth, the Universe, your body, and your life than you've probably ever paid attention to. All kinds of energy is moving around you at this very moment in time, and it changes minute to minute, day to day, week to week, and even year to year.

As an Empath, you possess an ability to "read" this energy, which means it can feel very unsettling and even chaotic to your spiritual or energetic body, especially when you are not aware of it.

Emotional energy (from other people) is definitely a part of this large Energetic Ecosystem; however, it's just a tiny piece to a very large puzzle. A puzzle that encompasses a world far beyond what the naked eye can see.

When you are unaware of the grandness of what this puzzle encompasses, and unaware of the Energetic Ecosystem, it makes it very easy (and typical) to focus upon what you "are" very aware of. Emotional Energy coming from other people. Especially because this involves the use of your physical senses, you can *see* people, you can *observe* people, you can *touch* people...

But the problem with focusing upon a very small piece of a larger puzzle is you only see a very small part of a larger picture. *Which means you're not properly equipped to work with and manage your energetic gift, as you don't have the proper knowledge or the proper tools.*

It's like someone saying to you, "Here's your map of the World, but it only has one country on it, sorry about that. Anyway, I want you to build a house by this river (not on the map). And here's your tools... You've got some wood and a hammer. Good luck!" Not only do you not have any knowledge about the other countries, rivers, or landscapes, but soon you find out you have no saw or nails... This seems like it will work out well, right?

When it comes to your Empath ability, without the proper knowledge and tools, it's no wonder you're not going to feel good. You need to know how to manage your energetic system.

Even if you could manage this little, tiny energetic portion (emotional or people energy) of your gift, what about the rest of the Energetic Ecosystem that you're ignoring and not really paying attention to? How's that being managed? How are you working with that? How do you manage to work with something that's not even being acknowledged?

If you are anything like I was, or even like most Empaths,

this is probably what's happening to you now... You're just trying to focus on one area. Not even aware of the other energetic rivers flowing around you, which can cause just as much havoc in the Ecosystem.

CHAPTER 2
The Energetic Eco System

The Energetic Ecosystem is where energy, atoms, and molecules all work together to create a bubble of life. *And it all stems from one source...energy...*

This vast system does not only include Earthly things and your reality, but it stretches far beyond anything the naked eye can see. It encompasses **all things.** It includes galaxies, universes, other planets, and the spirit realm, just to name a few.

These things are all made of energy, and energy does some very incredible things. There are two characteristics that you will want to pay very close attention to.

1) Energy binds all things together.
2) Energy is in a constant state of movement.

What's incredible about these two things is nothing else in existence does this. It's the nucleus and the hub of all things ever created, experienced, or even imagined...

However, because the Energetic Ecosystem is so vast, and

for the sake of this book, it's a good idea to focus on an area that directly affects your life.

Your mind, body, and spirit are all a part of the Energetic Ecosystem... It's what makes you, YOU...

Mind – Body – Spirit

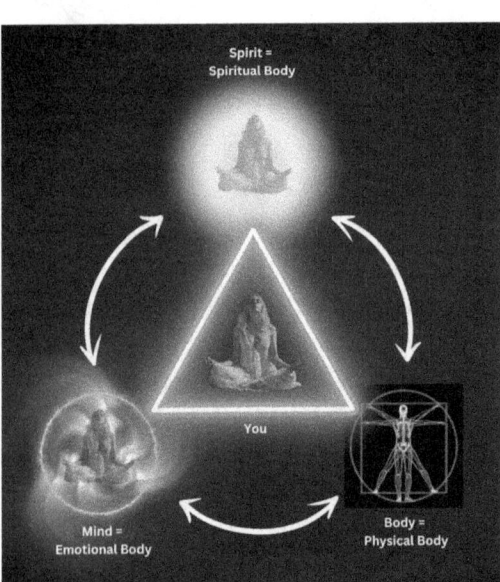

I feel like the term mind body spirit has lost its deeper meaning because of the watered-down information out there and the assumptions people make about what that means or entails. It's an overused term used to describe wellness. But wellness is not described by three words; it lies in the deeper meaning of the bubble of life.

From an energetic perspective, not only are you tied to all things energetically, but it's important that you allow energy to flow freely within your personal Energetic Ecosystem.

This is imperative information if you want to allow

wellness to become your dominant frequency. Because it's not a suggestion, it's required...

Energy needs to move and flow.

Flow and movement will allow new energy to move in and through you, creating new experiences. As well as clearing out old or unhealthy energy (toxicity) from your system. This and maintaining a higher frequency are the only way to obtain energetic wellness. And energetic wellness is required for your physical, spiritual, and emotional bodies to create a healthy physical reality. From a physical standpoint, this means good mental and physical health.

However, without this information, mainly people rely on what they've been told growing up or the information that's readily available in and about the physical world. How things work physically, such as:

- You work hard, you earn money.

- Your body can fail you, you can catch an illness, or a disease.

- There are limited opportunities, you better take what you can get, this is just reality.

These things all come from a physical-based mindset. This implies all things are not connected together, and energy plays no role in these outcomes. But this is not true; all things are connected and dictated by energy. So, with that in mind, here's the difference.

1) Money flows to those who allow it.

Money (currency) is an energy, but this also means it can be blocked. So the way you view money (mind = emotional body) and how you feel about money will direct the flow.

2) Your body doesn't fail you.

Your spiritual body and emotional body are made up of a frequency, and this frequency is filled with information on how the physical body creates cells, and how the organs and body parts are supposed to operate. Imagine it as if the spiritual body is a battery, and the emotional body is the owner's manual for your car—your physical body. All of the car parts can be there, but if the battery (spiritual body) is not in place, the car won't run at all. And if something goes wrong, we need to look to the owner's manual (the emotional body) to see what we need to adjust or fix. Your energetic system is the *only reason* your physical body operates.

3) Your reality (physical awareness) is created by how you feel (emotional body) and your belief system (spiritual body).

Opportunities are abundant; there are no limitations. Because energy is not limited, it is infinite, which means there are infinite possibilities. Way beyond what your physical brain can comprehend.

While this might seem like unimportant information, it's very important information for an Empath to have.

This is especially true because when you are born, energy is your first language.

It's the first thing you navigate as a baby with your spiri-

tual senses. Babies respond to all the energy around them. It's the language of the spirit realm, animals, plants, and nature. It's the dominant Universal Language. And it's natural to us...
We have to *learn* how to be physical.

- We learn how to talk, walk, touch and grab things.

- We learn taste, spicy and mild, hot and cold.

- We learn verbal language.

- We learn what smells belong to what, and what they mean.

- We learn to listen and compartmentalize what we are hearing.

That's also why babies can be easily startled. They are learning about physicality and learning how to be physical, because all they've known until they are born again is how to be an energetic being. This is what is the most natural and familiar to them. This is also why they respond so vigorously to emotions.

Someone who's looking at them with joy or yelling in anger will trigger a response because of the energy they are feeling, sensing, and reading. They don't know verbal language; they know energy, and they can read it very well. You have to learn verbal language and physical beliefs. This is also why you don't become as rigid in your mindset until you are older. You have to learn a physical belief system, and that takes time, several years in fact.

By the time you become an adult, you have rewired your brain completely to live a very physically based lifestyle. A lifestyle with physical rules. You are taught these rules in school, by your parents, teachers, and other influential adults. How it makes no sense to work with anything you can't see...your imagination, dreams, desires, abundance, infinite possibilities. You can't see these things, they don't exist, there's no physical proof!

Then you navigate through life like everyone else, until one day, you find out you're an Empath. Or you finally come to realize there's a lot more to life than the things you can see. That's when you search for answers or find yourself reading this book.

Which is amazing...because it's your first step to a whole new life. The one you've been waiting for. So let's begin the journey of relearning what you have forgotten, set aside, or trained yourself to ignore.

This is your first step to learning how to live your best life as an Empath.

CHAPTER 3
Common Misconception & Hurdles

Let's start digging into what this ability is really all about. There's a common misconception when it comes to an Empath ability. People believe that an Empathic ability is a separate ability (if they consider it an ability at all) from all the other psychic senses or Claires. But the thing is, it not only falls in the realm of being related to a psychic sense, but it's also part of the family. *It actually "is" one of the Claires, and one of your psychic senses.*

What are the different psychic senses? Let's cover that briefly for a moment because understanding where it lies in the psychic family tree is important.

Clairvoyance is clear seeing, which is the ability to receive psychic information visually by "seeing" spirits or energy with the naked eye, or the mind's eye.

Clairaudience is clear hearing, which is the ability to receive psychic information by "hearing" spirits or energy with the outer ear or inner ear.

Clairtangency is clear touch, which is the ability to receive psychic information through "touch" or touching an object.

Clairgustance is clear taste, which is the ability to receive psychic information through "taste." Typically, you can taste something without actually eating it and receive psychic information at that time.

Clairscent is clear scent, which is the ability to receive psychic information through "scent" or smelling an object. The scent will appear without any visual reason, or you can receive psychic information simply by smelling an object.

Claircognizance is clear knowing, which is where things get a little more complicated. It's the ability to receive psychic information through "a knowing" in the energetic body. That one trips people up because they don't understand how they can have a "clear knowing" of something they should not necessarily know.

Clairsentience is clear energy, which is even more complex than claircognizance. *It's the ability to receive psychic information through energy.* This is where your Empath ability lies, and why it's commonly referred to as being an Empath.

Now I want to point out something that you might find very interesting: most of the time your psychic senses primarily involve you working with one or more of your physical senses as well. You're seeing, hearing, touching, tasting, and smelling as a way to receive and perceive psychic information. Even claircognizance requires you to pay very close attention to feelings in the torso area.

It feels natural to use your physical senses in conjunction with your spiritual senses, but this also brings us to hurdle #1...

When you are working with clairsentience, or your Empath ability, it primarily involves working with your Spiritual Body and its senses.

Having an Empath ability is the easy part; you can feel energy without much effort. However, understanding it and managing it requires you to be very in tune with your spiritual/energetic body. And this can essentially become a major hurdle since most people are physical body dominant.

Physical body dominant refers to a person's tendency to prioritize their physical experiences, emotions, sensations, and needs over spiritual aspects.

Individuals who are physical body dominant often focus on things that are tangible, concrete activities such as exercise, health, or physical appearance. They search for fulfillment through their physicality, preferring hands-on experiences or activities that engage the physical body's senses such as sight, taste, touch, and smell. This dominance can sometimes lead to neglecting emotional or spiritual well-being, so it's important for individuals to strive for a balance among the three aspects —mind, body, and spirit.

When you are learning to work with your spiritual/energetic body, it can feel very much like unfamiliar territory, mainly because the essence of your spiritual body is not physically based but it is energetically based (which is why it's often referred to as the energetic body). Your energetic body is also the foundation of your existence, and because of the spiritual body's extensive energetic foundation, it naturally works within the parameters of the Energetic Ecosystem, as you learned in the last chapter.

This can make things incredibly confusing and hard because now you're dealing with something you can't see, yet energy is everywhere all the time!

It's not uncommon for Empaths to be confused or unaware of what's happening to them or around them. As an Empath, you're experiencing a lot of different feelings and reading an abundance of energy daily. And you've probably found yourself feeling like, *"I'm not really sure what's going on, but something is definitely happening."*

An Empath ability is one of the most confusing of all the psychic senses and absolutely one of the hardest abilities to cope with. Not just because this gift is vast and complex, but mainly because this gift is very misunderstood.

And when you do find information about this gift, it's taught in a very cookie-cutterish style. You are taught about that very small portion of the gift (emotional energy = one puzzle piece), and it leaves you wondering, *"Why am I still feeling this way? I still feel crappy!"*

If being an Empath meant you were just dealing with people and emotional energy because it was truly the heart of this gift, you'd feel better once you managed that part. You wouldn't even need to take any classes or educate yourself further. You'd be able to read things on the internet because that part of the puzzle is everywhere, and you'd feel better.

When you're missing information, it's very difficult to learn how to develop your gift, how to manage your gift, or how to work with it in general. Here's the issue: **it's one of the easiest abilities to tune into, yet one of the hardest abilities to manage by a long shot...**

That's what makes it one of the more confusing gifts, because you can tune into it very easily, even when you don't want to, unlike your other psychic gifts where you typically need to use a more focused approach.

For instance, I have all the abilities we just covered, and the amount of work it takes to manage my Empath ability vs. my other psychic abilities is not even close. It's like being a teacher and having all these really good students and then having one that's just causing havoc, running around, completely out of control the whole time. It's just crazy.

CHAPTER 4
Understanding Your Empath Ability

How does one become an Empath? It's simple. You are born with this ability; it doesn't just develop out of nowhere. It's just like your other psychic abilities; you are born with spiritual senses, just like you are born with your physical senses. Which means you are born with the ability to utilize your spiritual senses.

Now that doesn't mean that if you're born with the ability to utilize some of the psychic senses we talked about that you're going to have all of them, which is also confusing because you want to know where your gifts lie. Which gifts do you have? Not to mention the combinations are always different. You might be stronger in claircognizance, and your friend might be stronger in clairsentience, and you both might have a little clairaudience, and neither may have clairscent.

Many individuals who are born with an Empath ability tend to ignore or distrust their intuitive senses from a young age. From an early age you are taught to dismiss your feelings and question the validity of the things you are sensing, such as your psychic insights. However, just because you don't remember having these abilities as a young child doesn't mean they weren't and haven't always been a part of you and who you are.

It's actually more common for people to be unaware of their own gifts, failing to recognize spiritual signs and intuitive hits, and dismiss them as mere coincidences. However, if we dive deeper into those experiences, the ones you had when you were young, you will often remember instances from your past where your abilities manifested quite substantially and even effortlessly. But then again, they were most likely dismissed.

If you're just now discovering or becoming more aware of your Empath abilities, it's a strong indication that you're also going through what is called a spiritual awakening.

A spiritual awakening is the process of reconnecting with your true spiritual self and who you are on a soul level. This will include things such as past lives, spiritual experiences, and spiritual gifts. As you uncover this hidden aspect of yourself, you gain access to a myriad of tools and knowledge that can enrich your life.

Your psychic senses and Empath abilities are closely intertwined with your spiritual body. When you align and embrace both aspects of yourself, your abilities will become even stronger. It's like unlocking a vast spiritual warehouse, filled with unique tools that require relearning and care.

Understanding your spiritual abilities and their purpose is vital, especially for Empaths. You need to learn how to develop and manage them effectively. By developing your psychic senses as a whole, you can also develop your Empath abilities and integrate them into your daily life. This holistic approach enhances your overall well-being, both physically and spiritually.

Unlike other psychic abilities, **being an Empath is constant and ever-present.** Once you become aware of your gift, it only grows stronger. That's when it's time to harness this incredible power and develop it to its full potential.

But before embarking on this transformative journey, it's vital to understand the difference between Empath management and development. You must learn how to manage your Empath abilities first, to create a solid foundation. Only then can you enter the realm of development and unlock the true potential within.

Imagine joining a swim team without knowing how to swim, struggling with exhaustion, dehydration, and sunburn. Similarly, focusing on becoming an Empath without first learning to manage this gift can lead to similar feelings of feeling overwhelmed and being unprepared.

This is why it's important to take things step by step, starting with mastering the art of managing your abilities before diving into development. This is also what sets an Empath ability apart from the other psychic senses—it requires a foundation of management.

While we will get to that shortly. First, it's time to discover why you were chosen.

CHAPTER 5

Why You Were Chosen

Empaths are not the same as other people. Every individual is born with spiritual senses or psychic senses, in the same way that you're born with your physical senses. And each person is born with the ability to develop these spiritual gifts.

What's also important to know is your combination of spiritual gifts will be different than other people's. And how you work with that combination will be unique to you. Not only are you unique as far as your spiritual gifts go, but how far you can develop those gifts will also differ.

But here's the interesting thing: ***while everyone is born with spiritual senses, not everyone is born an Empath.*** Being an Empath is different. And this brings us to the first very important thing that you need to know.

Empaths are chosen.
You were chosen.

Most Empaths don't know how special they really are. They were specifically chosen by a spiritual council before birth.

This gift is very, very special. A council determines whether or not you are to receive your Empath gift, because Empaths have a very important job to do. But before we get into that, it's important to understand what makes an Empath's gift so special.

As an Empath you are born with a higher vibrational frequency than other people.

And this is huge for you to know because when you're chosen, you're spiritually wired a bit differently than other souls.

You are gifted with a heightened ability to feel and connect with all energy, which means you're also a natural conduit for different types of healing energy.

This is really important information. That does not make you better than other people. It makes you **different** than other people, and it makes this ability different.

It allows you the very unique and powerful gift of being able to work with energy—all energy. And that's where this gift lies, within your higher vibrational frequency. And this ability is strong.

You have a very special relationship with energy. Not only can you read energy, but energy naturally flows through you and will radiate outward. People and animals can feel this high vibe energy, which is what causes so many people to navigate and naturally gravitate towards you.

- They want to be around you.

- They want to talk to you.

- They want to get advice from you.

This energy that flows through your body feels good to those who are struggling, and they often feel better by just being in your presence. This brings us to the second important thing you need to know.

Empaths are born natural healers.

Being born with this higher vibrational frequency has a purpose; it makes you a healer. You are prewired with the ability to work with and navigate high-frequency energy through your spiritual and physical bodies in a way other people are not.

This is why many Empaths at some point in their lives find themselves thinking things like:

- I feel like I want to be a healer, but how can I tell if I have the gift of being a healer?

- I feel like I have a gift, but I'm unsure and I don't know what to do about it.

- Or if they think they have a gift, they think, what am I supposed to do with it?

- How am I supposed to know?

And even if you can't quite put your finger on why, you might find there have been or will be many points in your life when you have had a deep internal desire to heal. You're spiritually wired differently.

You have a higher vibrational frequency, which allows you to move energy differently than other people.

You ARE different. And that's what brings us to the third important thing you need to know.

Healing is a part of an Empath's purpose.

As an Empath, healing is part of your purpose and part of why you're here on Earth in this lifetime. More Empaths are being born right now than ever before, and there's a reason for this. It was all divinely timed for those of us who were chosen to receive this gift. We were chosen to help shift the vibration of the world and to help the world become a healthier place vibrationally when being called upon. And we are being called upon now...

This may seem like a lot and even overwhelming, but it is true. When I was a young Empath, I never ran across other Empaths. Although my gift was very strong, it was really hard to figure out my own gift because I had nowhere to go. Even my mentors didn't really understand the gift. There were hardly any books written on the subject, and it wasn't talked about; Empath knowledge was pretty much nonexistent.

This created an incredibly hard journey for me, I had to really navigate through this world alone and figure out how this gift worked and what made it different than the other gifts that I had. I knew I was born psychic, but being an Empath was a very different journey.

This unique gift did not behave in the same manner whatsoever, and I didn't even realize that it was my Empath ability that was causing my physical health issues. You assume as a young psychic, or being born very aware of your psychic senses, that they all work the same. Yet it became very clear to me that my other senses worked in a very different manner.

Before you get too overwhelmed from learning you're a healer and you were specifically chosen to help shift the vibration of the world, it's actually simpler than it sounds. Especially with some guidance...and this is where understanding what being a healer means can be really helpful.

A healer is someone who has a natural ability to raise another person's vibration, and that's it.

It really doesn't matter if it's one person or a whole group of people. As a healer, you have a natural ability to raise the vibrations of people you come into contact with. Whether you do that knowingly or unknowingly, ***when a person leaves your presence feeling better than they did before they arrived, that's the sign of a healer.***

Raising the earth's vibration one person at a time is just as important as trying to do a mass healing. Everyone does things differently, and healing can be done in several different ways. Healers all heal differently.

- Some healers make it a profession.

- Others seek out people who they think need healing.

- Some healers like to heal quietly, without anyone noticing.

- And sometimes healers like to work only with nature or animals.

- Some healers pretend they're not even healers at all.

- Other times they just let people naturally gravitate towards them.

The healing aspect of being an Empath is actually the easy part. However, that brings us to a very complex set of problems.

Empaths typically don't feel that great unless they've had some proper training.

As an Empath you won't typically feel very well unless you know what is happening. As you can tell so far, there's a lot that Empaths must manage. Which means there's also probably a lot more going on in your life than you initially thought about or realized.

Since you are prewired with a natural ability to heal, you are basically trying to heal everyone all the time, whether you are aware of your energetic intention or not.

Energetically, you will even do this with those who are not ready to be healed. This is why it's so important to understand how managing your gift is directly linked to your spiritual and physical health and your overall well-being. If you learn the wrong Empath management techniques or the right techniques in the wrong order, this can trip you up just as much as anything else.

However, the good news is you can feel well and even empowered because it's all about being fully prepared and knowledgeable to the best of your ability. You just need to take the time to build up your energetic strength and spiritual knowledge as an Empath, just like you would your physical strength and sports knowledge as a swimmer.

CHAPTER 6

Being an Empath vs Empathy: What's the Difference?

Somehow over the years people have taken the word Clairesentience and replaced it with the term Empath —which is fine, but I think it adds to the confusion. It's almost like people are trying to make it a category on its own, in a way. A category that's disconnected from your spiritual senses, which is why it can add to the confusion of being an Empath.

To add more confusion, we have empathy, which seems like a word that is very closely linked to being an Empath. So it's natural that people would assume, *Well, if I'm an Empath, I would have empathy*. And the funny thing is, a lot of Empaths do not necessarily have empathy, which I will also talk about.

So what is the difference between being an Empath and having Empathy?

Being an Empath is the ability to perceive and receive psychic information through energy.

Having empathy is the action of understanding, being aware of, and being sensitive to the feelings, thoughts, and experience of another.

The main difference is psychically receiving information through energy (psychic sense) vs. understanding and having an emotional response to another person's experience (emotional response).

These two things are very different. Mentally understanding and perceiving what somebody else is going through, and having a heartfelt moment for their situation, versus being able to actually feel what that person is feeling as if you're **experiencing the same emotional response within your own body** is not the same at all.

Let's talk about the mental aspect for a minute. Your brain will compartmentalize a lot of things when it comes to being in someone else's presence. You can hear the tone of their voice, you can see the look on their face, and you can watch their mannerisms. You can analyze somebody without even realizing you're doing it with your eyes, your ears, and other physical senses. This can make you feel sad for them, or feel like, *I'm really feeling upset that they are in this position.*

That is not being an Empath; that is being empathic.

Weirdly enough, Empaths often times will do the complete opposite of someone who is empathic. Because of the sheer volume of energy Empaths are exposing themselves to on a day-to-day basis, guarding themselves from other people's emotional energy that doesn't feel good to them can be an automatic response. They don't want to be engulfed in someone else's drama, problems, issues, or meltdowns.

It becomes a protection mechanism.

It's common for an Empath's initial response to be, *Oh, I don't like that feeling. I don't like that in my body. I don't like the way that that feels.* And the first thing they think of is to get away from it.

Empaths who are more aware of the energy they feel will tend to step away from any frequency that feels uncomfortable to them. Especially when it's unnecessary to subject yourself to something that doesn't feel good to you.

When you are an Empath, you can feel others' emotions in your own body. You can feel it in your own frequency, as if they are your own. That's an Empath. Which is very different than observing somebody.

And truthfully feeling someone else's emotions in your own body doesn't do anyone any good. An Empath merging themselves with another person's energy and mirroring their emotions serves no purpose except for in two different scenarios.

1) You are in healing mode:

You are using this ability to see beyond words and explanations to get to the root of what's happening within the emotional body of someone else for the sake of helping to heal them in some way.

2) For safety, protection, or awareness:

You are using this ability to see what someone's true intention is. True intention will show up in the emotional body of the other person. And it is there you can determine honesty and intention.

However, not all Empaths can compartmentalize what is happening. But if they are aware enough, they might just make a habit of stepping away from energy that doesn't feel good, realizing:

This situation doesn't feel good.
Something feels off.
I'm not feeling comfortable.
I've got to get out of here.

Which is why a lot of Empaths are reclusive. They might not want to help other people all the time. That energy can feel very heavy to them. This is why some Empaths think:

I can't be an Empath.
I'm not even empathic.
I don't feel for that person.
I don't want to be near that person.

This response feels very counterintuitive to the word Empath.

However, this response is another protective mechanism that many Empaths use to protect their energy.

If you're around somebody who has low energy or a heavy frequency for long periods of time, it can start to feel like your own frequency. It can feel like something you're resonating or experiencing. Something that's in your own body.

This is a very real thing and can happen if you're not careful.

When you do not know how to separate your frequency from others by practicing awareness and energy management techniques, you can pick up on a frequency from someone else and it can alter your own frequency.

How do you avoid this? You need to build up your energetic system. Similarly to how it's important to build muscle by lifting weights and exercising, your spiritual body needs to build energetic strength.

You must do things to protect your energetic system, clear your energetic system, and put a buffer between you and other people. Your goal is to make your energetic system stronger than the other people you might be around. The strength of your energy will trump the weakness of their energy, if that makes sense. It becomes too strong for their frequency to enter into your system.

I will talk about how to do that later, but first a little recap.

- Being an Empath and having empathy are not the same at all. One is a psychic sense, and one is a mental perspective.

- Not all Empaths have empathy. The ones who are more protective of their energy steer clear of heavy energy and emotional interactions. That can appear as having a lack of empathy, when it's actually a protective mechanism.

- Many Empaths are reclusive and particular about who they are around.

- Strong Empaths will typically want to protect their energy more than they want to help heal others. They want to be selective of who and when they help heal with words, energy, love, attention, etc., because there's an exchange of energy that takes place, and they can feel it. It affects them.

These are not selfish actions; they are smart actions. Because you must be a strong, healthy Empath before you help anyone else. Otherwise, you are not doing anyone any favors. And that's going to bring us to our next chapter.

CHAPTER 7
Empath Traits & Characteristics

Why is it important to understand Empath traits and characteristics? Because there are reasons behind them, and just like every other aspect of being an Empath, they all revolve around energy. When you understand why these characteristics can be triggered by your gift, it allows you to shift your perspective on why you do some of the things you do and what might be causing you to feel certain ways.

There are eleven main traits that I think you should be aware of. Don't focus too much on how many of these resonate with you; that's not the point. Most Empaths will find that they've struggled with many of these during their Empath experience. The point is understanding what might be normal for an Empath.

If you do, you won't feel as annoyed or frustrated with yourself, or feel if you are not as functional as other people in your life.

1) Empaths can be mentally hard on themselves.

I wanted to talk about this one first because unlike the other ones I will be talking about in this chapter, this one is often overlooked or even ignored.

Empaths can tend to have unrealistic or high expectations of themselves and become upset when they feel as if they failed this high expectation.

- They are often judgmental towards themselves when they can't do things they want to do or like other people can do.

- They often hold themselves to a higher-than-normal standard.

- They often become disappointed in themselves or feel like a failure if they fall short of these expectations, the ones they have set for themselves.

- They often see themselves as less than others who surround them.

Because an Empath has an innate ability to tune into all energy, they have a natural ability to feel source on a deeper level than other people. This deep connection often goes unnoticed because when you are bombarded with so much energy it's hard to sort through what you are feeling, so the awareness of knowing what it is they are feeling can be mute.

Within source energy there is greatness, love, and expansion. There is an unspoken knowing that you can achieve all the things in life you want to achieve. It's a deep knowing, but when you are physically focused, this knowing can cause discord.

It gets confused with the physical idea of success and greatness. Expectations are set, and that snowball will gain momentum as it rolls downhill. You strive to touch that feeling of expansion and possibilities from a physical standpoint, which can leave you feeling disappointed or even like a failure when that feeling does not manifest into a physical experience, and when you feel disappointed over and over again, that feeling of failure gains momentum.

The issue with this is source energy, the ever-expansive feeling of love, creation, joy, and expression are found within creation. Creation is your connection to source energy. And this cannot be found through a physical experience stemming from low vibrational frequencies or emotions.

In other words, you cannot start from a place of frustration, worry, or fear and create with source energy. It doesn't work. Those vibrational frequencies will never match. You must learn to change your life experience so you create from a place of a higher vibrational frequency.

But this usually requires making different choices in your life so you are not continuing to repeat your same habits and patterns over and over again. For example, releasing all low vibration emotions you are holding onto as quickly as possible when they appear in future experiences. It might also require you to make some adjustments to your energetic environment.

2) Empaths can be prone to feeling overwhelmed.

This is usually a side effect of how you are managing things energetically, or mismanaging things energetically. Here are a couple of ways it can show up for you as an Empath.

- Energy overload from your environment, chaotic energy, or even white noise can leave you feeling overwhelmed, which will automatically make you want to leave or try to calm the energy around you.

- High expectations that you put upon yourself or others can constrict energy, causing you to feel pressure as the energy is not flowing properly. It's constricted.

- Doing too many things at once. Empaths have this natural urge to help others, which usually results in them taking on too many things at once. Which oftentimes results in the next one.

3) Empaths can be prone to burn out.

Or basically running themselves into the ground. They feel the need to help everyone all the time because that's what they are wired to do—heal. And when someone is feeling upset or overwhelmed you can feel it and you want to help calm their energy.

- You are expected to help others. People are drawn to you as an Empath and those same people will create a habit of coming to you so you can make them feel better.

They expect it from you. They might need emotional support or physical support (helping pick someone up, do a task, etc.). When you are an Empath your first response is to help, but if you are not managing your energy properly, this will lead to burn out because you are giving away more of your energy than you are taking in.

- When you hold high expectations of yourself, or when others hold you to a high expectation, it's not uncommon for you to push yourself to the edge of your energy reserves.

You might not even realize you are doing it. If you don't realize you are getting close to your limit, because you think you can do everything all the time, you will hit a wall. Then you must take a break because recovery time is now essential.

This can be a huge problem with Empaths because they view saying no as if they are neglecting someone's needs. This is not the case at all; you are self-preserving. You cannot help everyone all the time, especially if there is no energetic return, otherwise, you will completely drain yourself to the point of burnout. Not to mention, usually people who won't drain you of all your energy are not asking you for help. They are more self-sufficient with their own time and energy.

When you don't take proper energy management techniques seriously and take time for self-care, you are neglecting your own needs. Taking time to recharge and rejuvenate your energy reserves keeps you healthy. It's not a weakness or self-indulgent; it's necessary.

4) Empaths are prone to feeling anxious.

This comes from many aspects of being an Empath, but again comes down to your ability to manage your energy and the energetic flow that surrounds you properly.

- You can feel anxious when you are placing high expectations on yourself, when you feel like you can't achieve what you want to.

- Being in the presence of certain people can make you feel anxious. You might find their energy feels weird or off.

- Negativity will definitely make you feel anxious. Negative energy doesn't feel good to an Empath. It can even make you feel physically nauseous or upset.

- You can feel anxious simply from the energy that surrounds you. Especially chaotic energy, which can stem from an environment or large groups of people, as the energy is moving every which way. Chaotic energy can also stem from a place of work or even a person who's all over the place.

Empaths need a calm, peaceful environment with a nice energy flow. This allows your system to relax. You can't constantly be in survival mode, but many Empaths are. They are having to protect themselves energetically every day. Protect themselves from negativity, toxicity, energy drain, and even their own resistance, which is based upon fear and worry.

However, you are also a product of your environment and the choices you make, and it's no different with energy. You create your own energetic environment, and you chose what energy to allow in your life. If it doesn't feel good to you, it's going to take some adjustment on your part.

5) Empaths are prone to overeating.

What many people don't know is the digestive process is a grounding process. The foods you eat will usually contain Earth energy. For example, vegetables, meats, and dairy are all products of Earth energy. When your body digests food, it does two things: it activates your grounding chakras, and you are also taking Earth energy directly into the body, which allows you to feel more balanced and calm. Because of this:

- Empaths often reach for food when they feel anxious or nervous.

- Your brain starts to correlate food with the sense of feeling calmer.

It's easy to see how it can become unconscious behavior, to reach for food when you are feeling unsettled or the energy around you feels overwhelming or chaotic. If you become aware of this, you can learn to be more aware of the last time you ate, and maybe take a walk outside instead, or use another grounding technique.

6) Empaths can be prone to addiction.

Simply for the fact that when you are using alcohol or other substances, it numbs your spiritual senses. When you don't understand energy and how it works, or understand how much of an influence it has over your spiritual and physical bodies, you can go into survival mode. And when you are in survival mode you will gravitate toward the fastest thing that will make this feeling stop.

- For some people that can be alcohol because of its ability to numb your spiritual senses, which allows you to block out energies better.

The bad news with this is not only does it make you way

more susceptible to lower vibrational frequencies, but your abilities can also be more amplified the next day, causing a vicious cycle of numbing them again.

Alcohol causes imbalance within your spiritual body and lowers your vibrational frequency. But it's all about moderation. If you can manage your alcohol intake when you are energetically taking care of yourself, you will just have a dip in balance and frequency, then you will balance back quickly.

But if you are using alcohol as a way to cope or numb your senses as an Empath, *as a way block out energy*, this is going to create quite an issue. Especially because the numbness is only temporary.

7) Empaths are prone to being obsessive.

When you can feel energy and it doesn't feel as if it's flowing properly, things will feel chaotic or stuck. And when something doesn't feel right or good to you, you can become obsessive about it.

- When energy feels chaotic, you will look to organize or compartmentalize thoughts, feelings, and emotions.

You can end up obsessing over emotions because you think you need to figure out a way to iron them out and make the energy of those emotions feel better. The issue with this is now you are hoarding your emotions, which doesn't work very effectively. The proper way to handle these emotions is to let them go...

If those emotions are tied to this very moment in time, then it's okay to take time to sort through them.

The majority of the time, however, this is not the case. Those emotions are usually low vibration emotions that are tied to a past experience or a future outcome. These emotions do not belong anywhere in your energetic system—that's only going to cause you issues. When you hoard emotions, you are just keeping a frequency alive and active within your system. You are not resolving it in any way.

- Empaths can also be obsessive about systems. They might have a certain system or way of doing things and they don't want to do it any other way.

Systems can make you feel like you are organizing energy, in a sense. When you create a system, you are essentially organizing a way for flow to happen. It might even just be because you are calming yourself emotionally, which allows flow to happen. Or you might have a physical or visual system which allows energy to flow more properly.

- Empaths can be obsessive about their environment and how it feels or looks. Again, this is a very visual way to establish flow.

Usually when an Empath is obsessive, they are trying to control the energy that surrounds them. They are trying to manage or control their own energy, their energetic environment, and the energy they come into contact with. Unfortunately, control is an ineffective way to attempt to calm your environment.

8) Empaths can be sensitive to white noise.

White noise is extensive background noise, and during the day white noise is at its peak. What Empaths don't notice or think about is this noise is not just determined by volume; it holds a frequency. And when you start to experience a lot of white noise at once, it also means you are experiencing a lot of frequencies at once, and it can be overwhelming.

- At a place of work, there can be a lot of white noise: people talking, doors moving, people coming and going.

- When you are out and about, there can be a lot of white noise: cars driving by, horns honking, people talking, electronics beeping, cash registers, doors opening and closing. Your awareness is heightened, and your sensitivities are up.

- When you go out to eat or socialize, white noise can become intense. If there are a lot of people around, or people drinking alcohol, music playing, the intensity can hit higher peaks than normal, especially because these things usually happen in an enclosed space, which contains this energy. In an outside space it's a lot easier to cope because the energy is free flowing and not so condensed.

- At home you are probably more affected by white noise than you think: kids running around, TVs on, music playing, microwave, washer, drier, phone, people talking, lawn mowers, or dogs barking.

You will want to pay particular attention to your home environment, because when you are in other environments white noise tends to be more on your radar. When you come home, you view that as your sanctuary. But home can have just as much white noise as other places, allowing you to feel tenser than you realize.

9) Empaths can be sensitive to electronics.

The electromagnetic waves produced by electronics are very noticeable when you are sensitive to energy. What you might not realize is these waves can cause you to feel edgy, moody, and irritated.

- Empaths have to be careful about working on electronics for long periods of time and not taking any time to ground themselves. Earth energy is the best tool for balancing this type of energy overload.

- Because of how vast and expansive your energy becomes at night, your sensitivity levels are on the higher side when it comes to electronics. This means it's not a good idea to have things like computers in your room at night or spend too much time on them before bedtime.

Because of the sheer amount of time you can spend on your computer or phone, and their closeness or proximity to your energy field, they tend to be the most problematic for Empaths.

10) Empaths can be prone to being night owls.

This one is fairly common and easy to explain.

- White noise is a lot lower at night.

Everyone tends to settle down. People go to sleep, they are winding down for the day, so there's less driving, talking, yelling, and less activity in general. This has a profound effect on the overall frequency volume of white noise, which feels very good as an Empath.

- The veil is thinner at night, which means that spiritual energy is on the higher side.

White noise is essentially static interference when it comes to connecting with spiritual energy. White noise is compiled of lower vibrational frequencies. At night when spiritual energy (high-frequency energy) becomes more apparent, you experience a greater sense of calmness. The energy feels lighter and more relaxing.

Because you can feel a shift in energy from day to night, not only will you experience more calmness, but you may also tend to be more energized at night. White noise, daytime dynamics, and environments tend to be very draining for an Empath. All the interaction, emotions, and noise can be very taxing on your system. At night your body is preparing to recharge, spiritual energy is on the higher side, and your energy is more protected with little effort.

11) Empaths can be prone to being moody.

When you are bombarded with energy all the time and you are not really paying much attention to your gift or what might be happening in your energetic environment, you can easily become moody.

- Energy will have a profound effect upon your mood. And if you don't learn how to approach your gift with awareness, you can have way too much energy coming at you all at once.

- You need to be aware to compartmentalize, because this is the only way to separate outside energy from your own. You need to be able to notice it, categorize it, and release it.

- If you don't learn how to compartmentalize and release energy, you will align with it.

And you don't want to align with outside energies of any kind. You will run the risk if you don't take a preventative approach. White noise, emotional energy from other people, it doesn't matter what form the energy comes in; if you are around it long enough your own vibrational frequency will try and adapt. Adapting to a lower vibrational frequency allows more flow than living in resistance.

Here are some common things to watch for that will trigger moodiness:

- When your energetic environment feels unsettled.

- When you're around low vibrational people, places, or experiences.

- When you are in a restaurant or socializing with energy that doesn't feel good or becomes overwhelming.

- When you are in a crowd.

- When you are around too much white noise or electronics for too long.

- When you are around too much white noise or electronics for too long.

- When you put too much pressure on yourself.

- When you are around people who are drinking or in a bar.

- When you are expected to help others.

- You can also tend to be moodier in the daytime than at night.

CHAPTER 8
What Kind of Empath Are You?

I figured this would come up at some point in time, so I wanted to make sure to include it. Some people believe that there are different types of Empaths. If you look on the Internet, or you google anything that has to do with Empaths at all, you've probably run across either a quiz, a podcast, or an article that says, *What kind of Empath are you?* Are you more drawn to nature? Are you really upset when you're around people? Are you this? Are you that? Are you drawn to animals? And then they say, *Okay, here's the type of Empath that you are.*

This can definitely cause some issues, so I want to address this question because I want you to become an Empowered Empath and not get sidetracked by information that is counterintuitive to that taking place.

First, I want to address the issue or the question, which is, are there different types of Empaths? No, absolutely not.

There are not different types of Empaths. There are different stages of Empath development.

And that's a very different thing. Not to mention, labeling just causes problems. First of all, it's inaccurate because **all Empaths have the ability to read all energy**, not just in one area or another. And that's why I don't like anyone labeling themselves an Emotional Empath or Nature Empath, it not only puts limitations on your gift, but you start training yourself to adhere to limiting beliefs, which do not belong anywhere in the Energetic Ecosystem. That just adds another hurdle.

However, it's entirely normal for Empaths to find it easier to read some energy and not others, especially if they've had no training.

You may know other Empaths, such as friend of yours or a family member, who find it easy to tune into emotional energy or emotions of other people. And maybe you find that you can tune into earth energy or animal energy really well. That doesn't mean you will never be able to read emotional energy and the other person will never be able to read earth energy or animal energy.

It doesn't mean that you don't have the same gift and ability to read energy—and this is where labeling causes problems. It really has nothing to do with if you have this gift and another person has that gift when it comes to the Empath gift itself. *It simply has to do with different stages of development or what energy you've trained yourself to focus on.* It just means you've learned to focus on a particular type of energy.

Labeling causes blocks. And I don't just mean with your Empath ability, but when you begin labeling any of your psychic senses and abilities, it tends to cause blocks and enhance limitations.

Blocks are a super common problem for those who "label" their abilities.

It makes people feel as if their abilities are cut and dried. They have this gift but don't have that gift, which doesn't allow for proper development with your other spiritual senses.

When you are developing one gift, it will have a domino effect on your other gifts as well. Over time, your other abilities will naturally begin to heighten, because they are tied together. They are a part of a "greater whole."

Some gifts you didn't even know you had might appear, and others that you thought were "minor" gifts are now "major" gifts.

I have people who will come to me and say, "I'm clairvoyant," or, "I'm clairaudient," and not even realize that they have a lot of other gifts underlying there.

For instance, they might also be an Empath, claircognizant, or have mediumship tendencies, but because they're very focused upon the label of what they think they're the strongest in, it tends to shift everything that direction, which can lead to blocking out some of the other gifts they may have. They may end up simply ignoring other abilities and not focusing on developing their psychic senses as a whole, which can be an issue because your spiritual (psychic) senses always work together. And hardly anybody has just one gift.

We all have a different combination of gifts. Your gifts are going to be different than your friends or your family members, but regardless of what gifts you have, they will want to work together. ***The whole point is working together.***

And truthfully, humans are the ones who put the labels on this stuff. People like to label things. The brain wants everything to have a label to help it organize, categorize, and compartmentalize. To basically make sense of things.

To help the brain with compartmentalization, you need to make sure you feed it the best knowledge you can, and it starts with understanding how your spiritual senses all work together as a package; they are a package deal.

JENNIFER O'NEILL

The first step is shifting your perspective, and seeing your senses as a package, not as individual units.

CHAPTER 9
Five Types of Empath Energies

As you know, those who have Empath abilities are born with them, but just like all of your other spiritual senses, there are different stages of development.

Even when you have the ability to read energy, energy itself has different strengths and behaves differently.

These strengths will normally correlate with different stages of your development. So let's talk about energy for a minute...

There are five different types of energy that you will work with as an Empath. It's good to know and learn and understand what these are.

Five Types of Empath Energies

Type 1 - People Energy (Very Strong Energy/Easy to Read) ~ *Such as people (live energy)*

People energy is very strong, which makes it harder to ignore than a lot of the other energies that you encounter. It's not just the strength of this energy that makes it the easiest to read, but you get visual feedback.

A look, tone of voice, appearance, and even experience via exchanging of energy between you and another person. This makes it a kind of *in-your-face* type of energy. Not to mention, people energy carries strong intentions or messaging behind the energetic exchange. Intention, words, telepathy, and emotions are all super powerful frequencies. *It's referred to as live energy because its strength and it's consistently moving.*

Type 2 - Earth Energy (Strong Energy/Somewhat Easy to Read) ~ *Such as nature, plants, animals, points on earth, cities, rocks, and landscapes.*

Earth energy is strong energy yet subtler than people energy in the sense that it's not typically so directive.

This energy creates a oneness when it comes to nature, the earth, and animals, as these frequencies are very much the same. This creates a link and interweb of energy that is consistently moving between all these things. And this frequency is directly connected to source or life energy.

Because it's not only environmental but also live energy, it's somewhat easy to read. Especially since you use your physical senses daily such as touch, sight, and smell.

However, it may take a little bit more focus on your part to tune into this type of frequency, as many people do not take the time to connect with it. It's common in this day and age to be primarily focused upon "white noise" for the majority of your day, such as your phone or television, driving, or what's going on around you at work, shopping, etc.

While this is common, white noise also hinders your connection to energetic frequencies making them harder to feel and read. So, when you are learning and developing the ability to connect with other frequencies, you will need to learn how to buffer yourself from this outside static while practicing.

Type 3 – Spiritual Energy (Strong Energy/Hard to Read) ~ *Such as information from the divine, spiritual realm, telepathy.*

Spiritual energy is strong energy but harder to read until you've become more accustomed to your spiritual body and trained or developed your spiritual senses to a certain point. This is when you must rely upon your spiritual and psychic senses to help you connect and tune in to this frequency. And since you typically will not be receiving any visual assurance or feedback, it's super easy to dismiss as nonexistent.

People are always looking for physical proof or visual proof when it comes to "compartmentalizing" something in your brain. If you don't see it, it didn't happen. This is purely because you've not given the brain enough knowledge to compartmentalize a spiritual energy experience. Something you feel with your spiritual senses vs. something you see with your physical senses, such as information from the divine or spiritual realm, but because it's hard to read, it will take more focus on your part.

Type 4 – Universal Energy (Strong Energy/Harder to Read) ~ *Such as lunar energy, star energy, universal energy, dimensional, and astral energy.*

Universal energy is strong and harder to read. Yet this energy has a very strong influence on your life.

While many Empaths can feel the influence, it's also one of the harder energies to read. Universal energy has laws it must follow, and it's dictated by things such as lunar energy, star energy, dimensional and astral energy. It will shift and change depending upon the position and energy of the planets, stars, earth's frequency, people's intentions, even your own thoughts and emotions.

It's pretty powerful because it encompasses most all things. One of the coolest things about Universal energy is you can learn to direct it and work with it. You are hard-wired to feel and recognize Universal energy, and it plays a major role in your life experiences.

Type 5 – Physical Energy (Somewhat Strong Energy/Very Hard to Read) ~ *Such as objects and physical items (imprint energy).*

Physical energy is somewhat strong, and it's very hard to read. Physical energy is attached to objects and physical items. It is also called imprint energy.

What that means is its energy that's left on a physical item and sort of sticks there. It's energy that adheres to a physical item and is carried with it until it's cleaned or cleared from the object.

Frequencies are filled with information. Experiences, memories, emotions and feelings, and intentions. When it comes to physical energy and imprints, the frequency that attaches itself to an object or physical item are typically connected to the past. The past of who's been there, who's touched it, etc. The energy is then left behind, as the source of the energy imprint is no longer there.

Since the energy is not as strong, it becomes very hard to read. This type of energy you will find in an antique store, estate sale, archeological sites, places of historic events, buildings, etc.

So how does all this tie together? How strong an Empath ability *feels* will normally correlate with the energy you are reading.

For instance, people energy may feel stronger to you than the energy of a place. Or nature energy might feel stronger than animal energy, etc. I'm going to talk about these different categories so you can see all the different types of energy you might experience on a day-to-day basis.

Most likely some of these categories will resonate with you more than others. For instance, people energy will almost always feel stronger to you than the energy of a place, or even nature. However, it's important to remember that as an Empath, you have the ability to tune into all energy at any given time.

Now, where your focus is and how you do that is going to depend on a lot of factors, and development will be one of them.

CHAPTER 10

Twelve Types of Empaths & Empath Labeling

I want to make sure I educate you on the full spectrum of Empath abilities. To do that, I will have to address the "labeling" portion which, as I already mentioned, I am not fond of. But this labeling is front and center when it comes to talking about Empaths. While I strongly suggest you steer away from labeling, it's also super important to know how and where the labeling comes from.

I believe it started from not fully understanding how an Empath ability works. It seemed like a helpful technique for some people to compartmentalize the things they were feeling. It helped give these feelings an identity. What I don't think people understand is that while compartmentalizing is important, it can also be very limiting. And when you put yourself in a small box, it's hard to control, maintain, and understand something that fits in an astronomically larger box.

I'm going to break these labels down into categories starting with the different types of energy to help you understand your Empath ability better. That will help you to make the correlation between what energy you are reading and why you might "identify" as a particular type of Empath.

TYPE 1 – PEOPLE ENERGY (Easiest to Read)

Emotional Empath

This is the label people most commonly associate with being an Empath. Emotional Empaths are known for sensing and feeling the emotions of others.

Emotional Empaths experience the emotions other people are feeling. You essentially "mirror" one's emotions. This can become very apparent when you meet someone new or when you can "feel" someone being dishonest with you.

The reason this one is most commonly associated with Empaths is because *you are essentially reading type 1 energy or people energy*. And if you remember it from the last chapter, it's the easiest energy to read.

This doesn't make you an *Emotional Empath*. It means you have ***a stronger ability to read people energy***. You're reading live energy, feeling what energy they are emitting, and receiving information based upon that frequency.

Medical Empath

Which brings us to our next label, a Medical Empath. Medical Empaths are described as being able to feel other people's aches, pains, and illnesses.

Feeling this energy might feel like intuitive awareness, like you are sensing the symptoms someone else has, or you may even feel the same physical symptoms or pains in your own body.

Tuning into someone's emotional or physical body and being able to feel ailments is fairly common with family members, especially with your own kids. You might also feel or see blockages in a person's energy field or be able to sense when energy is not flowing properly throughout the body or the chakra system.

People who might think of themselves as Medical Empaths would be moms, as they tend to be really tuned into their own children. Also, people in the healing field, whether they knowingly or unknowingly think about it, such as nurses, Reiki practitioners, doctors, or anyone in the traditional or wholistic medical fields. If they are tuned in, often times they can sense disruption in people's energy, which can cause health issues.

Being able to energetically tune into medical issues essentially means you've trained yourself to tune into *people energy* on a deeper level. This allows you to be able to see and feel how that energy is flowing through the body.

TYPE 2 – EARTH ENERGY (Medium to Read)

Animal Empath

An Animal Empath commonly refers to someone who can tune into the thoughts and feelings of the animal life around them. They have a sense of what an animal is feeling, experiencing, or might need.

They tend to have a very deep connection with almost all animals and find they have a very hard time going to zoos, the circus, or anywhere animals might be caged or treated poorly. It could even be at someone's house or anywhere you see an animal confined in some way.

This means you've trained yourself to tune into *earth energy*, on a deeper level than others. If this is you, if you really pay attention, you will start noticing it's not just animals that you usually can tune into. You've developed or are developing a strong connection to earth energy, and you can learn how to broaden that part of your development.

It's common for people who connect with animals and

earth energy to become vets, groomers, horse riders, animal communicators, or they might even just be animal lovers.

Nature or Plant Empath

Along these same lines of working with ***earth energy*** we have the labeling of Nature Empaths or Plant Empaths.

Nature Empaths have strong connections with nature or essentially earth energy, which includes plants, trees, rocks, and anything nature related. Typically, those who love being in nature label themselves Nature Empaths. They can naturally tune into the energy around plants. This can help to create highly skilled gardeners as they can sense what a plant needs to thrive.

However, I am a very strong earth energy reader, and I am not a highly skilled gardener, so don't think you need to be skilled for this to be you. People who identify as a Nature Empath might also find they have a strong need or desire to help protect the earth and its environment.

If you connect with earth energy you might feel strongly about things such as recycling eco-friendly products and buying organic. Environmentalists would typically be strong empaths who identify with being labeled a Nature Empath. But again, remember if you identify with being a Nature Empath, it means you have a naturally gifted ability to tune into earth energy. However, when you take out the labeling, you might find that you can also tune into people energy as well.

I hope you can see a pattern emerging here, and I hope this will encourage you to want to know how to become an Empowered Empath, getting rid of tedious labels. This will allow you to let go of being put in a little category labeled in a box, and you'll realize that your true ability is much broader, on a much grander scale.

Crystal Empath

Next, we have what people like to call a Crystal Empath. These are people who feel a powerful connection to crystals and gemstones, which again indicates a natural ability to tune into **earth energy**. They can feel a different vibration coming from the stones when holding them in their hands, wearing them, or placing them in a room.

Empaths who are connected to crystals and gemstones can greatly benefit from their calming energy. Although this is not always the case, people who feel very connected to earth energy through crystals might notice all kinds of physical sensations. They might feel hot when they hold them or feel a tingling sensation.

For those who are drawn to crystals but might not feel any physical sensations, it doesn't mean you are not benefiting from the energy they project and circulate. You're still benefiting from their energy—earth energy. It helps to calm your own energetic system and even helps with aligning your system to the frequency of the earth, which is extremely beneficial.

Even if you can't feel the vibration coming from them, if you're drawn to them, it's a very good indication that you need some alignment with earth energy and or maybe you're not connecting with earth energy as much as you should be. So it's a good thing to be aware of when it comes to crystals.

TYPE 3 – SPIRITUAL ENERGY (Hard to Read)

Spiritual or Medium Empath

Spiritual Empaths feel strongly connected to the spiritual realm and **spiritual energy**. They can feel guides, angels, ancestors, and loved ones connected to themselves or others.

They can experience the feelings, thoughts, or mental impressions of those in the spiritual realm. Spiritual Empaths are very interested in anything which has to do with the spiritual world or a higher power.

Even if you've not quite developed your ability yet, if you feel the urge to connect with these higher frequencies you probably fall into this category. This means it's time to learn how to develop your energetic connection to the spirit realm.

This is where some of your other gifts will come into play, you can use them to help gather knowledge and information. Those gifts are valuable tools when it comes to helping you communicate with those in the spiritual realm.

Intuitive or Claircognizant Empath

Next, we're going to move to the label of Intuitive or Claircognizant Empath. This is going to be very similar to a Spiritual Empath. Intuitive or Claircognizant Empaths have a strong ability to tune into *spiritual energy*.

This allows you the ability to gather a lot of information from someone by simply being in their presence. If you are one of these people you might find it easy to feel the energy and intentions behind a person.

You may also have a "knowing" and understanding of someone's past, present, and even past life experiences.

This one is interesting because when you are dealing with a person on a more advanced psychic level, you're essentially tuning into *people energy and spiritual energy at the same time*, but you're also using a lot of your other spiritual and psychic senses as well.

You use these senses as a part of a package to gain knowledge, not just of the spiritual realm, but knowledge of things that might have happened in the past, or even in another lifetime. When you do this, it allows you to have access to all kinds of spiritual knowledge. This takes some training and development.

TYPE 4 – UNIVERSAL ENERGY (Harder to Read)

Lunar Empath

Universal energy is definitely hard to read. A Lunar Empath is referring to someone who is strongly connected to lunar and planetary energy. They can be extremely affected by lunar cycles, such as full moon, new moon, and even solar eclipses.

They are also sensitive to other planetary movements, such as retrogrades and other changes. If you identify with this type of energy, you might also call yourself a moonchild.

However, there's a lot more to it under the surface than you might recognize. It's not just being an Empath who resonates strongly with universal energy.

This means most likely you've spent a lot of other lifetimes working with lunar energy and you can access that knowledge by learning how to align with universal energy.

Learning how to align with any of the energies we've been talking about allows you to create a relationship with your spiritual body and gain awareness that might have been overlooked before.

It also helps the brain to compartmentalize and create a space for knowledge that is coming from another realm or place it can't validate with your physical senses. It helps the brain understand and create a relationship with your spiritual body and recognize one of its great capabilities. It creates a conduit to all the frequencies that hold unlimited amounts of knowledge and understanding that we are not privy to in the physical world.

Astral Empath

This brings us to another gift that also works with space and *universal energy*—an Astral Empath, also known as a starseed or starchild. An Astral Empath is someone who feels strongly connected to other beings and dimensions.

If you identify with being an Astral Empath or starseed, you might find you have the ability to feel other dimensional beings, such as fairies, extraterrestrials, and even other planetary worlds. You might be very drawn to sci-fi movies such as *Star Wars*, *Thor*, *Dune*, or even films such as *Divergent*.

Astral Empaths strongly remember and recognize live energy on other planets. And most likely you've lived many lives on other planets. Some Astral Empaths feel other planetary energy so strongly they become homesick. They tend to be more aligned with star energy than earth energy, hence the name starseed or starchild.

You've also lived more lifetimes on other planets than you've lived here on Earth. This can cause you to feel a little bit disconnected from earth energy and even sometimes people energy. And more connected to *spiritual energy and universal energy*.

Telepathic Empath

The typical description of a Telepathic Empath is one who can feel other people's thoughts. More commonly, Telepathic Empaths have a deeper knowledge and understanding of the energy of your thoughts and how this energy can manifest into physical energy and experiences, essentially creating one's reality. This is *universal energy* at its finest...

If you identify as a Telepathic Empath, you also tend to be very good at working with manifestation and the law-of-attraction techniques. Most likely you are drawn to anything having to do with universal laws and universal energy. Most all Empaths are strong manifesters, born with this underlying knowledge and understanding of how energy works. It's just learning how to recall and find this information. Then teach your brain how to compartmentalize properly as well as how these energies work.

TYPE 5 – PHYSICAL ENERGY (Hardest to Read)

Geomantic Empath

An example of someone who reads *physical energy* would be someone who identifies as a Geomantic Empath. Geomantic Empaths identify with feeling the energy left behind in a specific place, or they might be drawn to certain places, such as churches, or places relevant to a historical event, such as Stonehenge, or the Roman Coliseum.

If you are one of these people you might also notice being drawn to strong energy points on earth. There are a lot of points on earth that radiate incredibly strong energy.

You may feel an affinity for places like sacred mountains, the Egyptian pyramids, Machu Picchu, Hawaii. When people come to Hawaii, they're just like, *wow, the energy here is incredibly different.* There's a strong healing energy presence, and a very strong energy point on earth.

Psychometric Empath

Another example of working with *physical energy* would be a Psychometric Empath. A Psychometric Empath receives impressions from inanimate objects, such as furniture, jewelry, photographs, or clothing.

For those who are untrained, this energy might feel dirty or uncomfortable on your hands if you touch an object, and sometimes even on your body if you are near an object. This is because when people handle items, they leave an energetic imprint. Depending upon the person or how the items are cared for, this energetic imprint can feel murky, dirty, or messy. This energy or frequency will also carry information. This is what you feel when you pick up one of those items.

It's super common for those who identify with being a Psychometric Empath to have trouble going into stores such as a pawnshop, thrift stores, or handling used items that don't belong to them.

However, just because you can feel it doesn't mean you have an understanding of what or where that energy resonated from or why it's stuck to that particular item. This takes more training. When you can't filter through this information, you can steer clear of that experience.

The good news is this energy can be cleared by washing one's hands, which is good to know if you ever find yourself dealing with used items or things like that.

When it comes to Empath energies or Empath types, there's no right or wrong, besides the fact that labeling can cause limitations. It doesn't mean that if you're very connected to universal or physical energy, that you're further than someone who finds it easier to connect with people energy or earth energy. It just means you're most drawn to those areas, *that energy is pulling you in and connecting with you.*

Energy does have characteristics, such as being weaker, or stronger; it may even be a little aggressive at times. When stronger energy or somewhat aggressive energy becomes more apparent to you and your frequency radar, you will find it easier to read.

Once you develop a relationship with that energy type, and get comfortable with it, such as how it works, and its energetic traits, then you will typically be moved or nudged towards another type of energy you are not so familiar with. This may be a nudge by your guides or the urge to development more. This is all a part of the domino process.

Focusing on that new, unfamiliar territory can help you create a more solid foundation, and stronger relationship with that new energy, which helps you become a stronger Empath and more empowered.

When it comes to developing any of your psychic senses, you will want to start with the area that you're feeling the strongest in and you are drawn to the most.

The same goes for your Empath abilities. You should focus on the energies you find the easiest to read or tune into, then allow spiritual expansion to take place on its own. Be open to expansion, development, and all possibilities.

We've covered a lot so far, and you should have a pretty good understanding of your Empath ability and why you were born with this gift in the first place.

Now it's time to get into the nitty gritty. **You can no longer live your life like other people...**

CHAPTER 11

Resistance & Acceptance

Learning how to feel better as an Empath is basically going to start with this chapter. This is when we start the process of lowering, or better yet, learning how to stop our resistance, which is extremely important.

It's common for Empaths to create a relationship with resistance. They use it to protect themselves energetically or try to control an outcome. This is mostly done by default, because in the physical world it's natural to try to stop something that doesn't feel good, feels overwhelming, or is too intense.

Let's talk about The Law of Resistance from an energetic standpoint for a moment.

From a Universal Law perspective, the Law of Resistance dictates that anything offering resistance will result in energy blockages or stuck energy.

As someone who's born with the ability to read and work with energy, this is exactly opposite of what we want to happen. When you are working with energy, you want to promote flow and fluidity. Healthy energy needs to flow and be in movement all the time.

When energy becomes stagnant or pools, it becomes toxic. The frequency lowers and there's no way to renew this energy until it's in movement. When energy moves, the frequency adjusts by allowing any old or toxic energy to flow or move away from a source while allowing the space to receive new, vibrant, healthy energy.

The key is to know where to look, so you can promote proper energetic flow, and not do the opposite by default or on accident.

Resistance normally shows up in an Empath's life in two ways.

1) When you are trying to protect your energy.

Trying to protect your energetic space from outside energy that doesn't feel good to you.

2) When trying to control an outcome,

By trying to be "normal" and do things that other people do while resisting the notion that you are different than other people.

Most everyone struggles with resistance. In fact, many people make this a lifestyle. However, as an Empath you need to be able to recognize when it's happening and understand that it may be causing you some difficulty.

An Empowered Empath lifestyle starts with acceptance, accepting that you're not the same as other people. If you're just discovering that you're an Empath, accepting that you are no longer the same as other people is part of the process, and it's imperative.

You are not the same as other people.

1) First, you discovered you were an Empath.

2) Next, you were taught why you were specifically chosen to receive your gift.

3) Now it's even more important for you to understand... *You can no longer live your life like other people.*

> *As an Empath you cannot do things like other people if you want to feel well.*

If you want to feel well, living your life like regular people is just not an option. Trying to be normal creates a huge problem for Empaths. It's a struggle because you want to feel well, but you also want to be normal, because normal people just seem to have things so much easier.

- They don't need to take the time to "prepare" themselves before going out.

- They don't need to "think" about who they're going to be around or what the energy is going to be like.

- They don't need to be "selective" when it comes to friends or who they hang out with.

- They can go into different places and experience no "aftereffects."

- They can enjoy large crowds without being "overwhelmed."

- They don't need to "ground" themselves when they get home.

- They can easily "ignore" the energy which surrounds them.

Normal people possess a different ability than you do. They have an ability to ignore energy or put blinders on when it comes to people or friends who may be toxic or feel negative to them. This means going out and doing normal things doesn't seem to have the same type of effect on their bodies or their physical and spiritual well-being.

- They can go into different places and experience no after-effects.

- They don't tend to feel the energy that was left in a room, a restaurant, a shop, or someone's house. They don't tend to feel the vibe so much unless it's super, super intense.

- They don't usually have a lot of problems going into different places.

- They can enjoy large crowds without feeling overwhelmed.

They don't experience the same results when they are being flooded with strong energy. To be fair, they may notice, however, because they are not wired the same, it's a lot easier for them block out or ignore energy. Their energy is primarily physically dominant, which means they are not wired to receive energy the same way. We can't do that; we are **wired to receive energy.**

The difference between you as an Empath and a normal person is there's a very dense layer of physicality between a normal person and energy in movement. Body mass, resistance, a belief system that revolves around being a physical being on a physical planet with very physical rules. While all things are energy, this combination creates a very thick, stagnant wall of energy that encompasses a normal person. And this wall blocks outside energy in movement. Instead of allowing outside energy to flow through and around the body, it promotes stagnant energy. Energy that pools. When energy is blocked or accumulating in one area with no flow, there's no energetic exchange.

As an Empath you are the polar opposite of a normal person as far as energy is concerned. Not only do you have the ability to read energy and connect with energy (as an energetic conduit), but your body is literally built to move and work with energy that's created outside the body and moves within the entire energetic ecosystem.

This energy is very fluid coming into your system and moving about your system, and even if you've never understood what it is you are feeling before, you're very aware of its presence. It's your natural ability, and it's a naturally occurring process.

But when you're normal, without an Empath ability, you don't have the extra special gift of being wired to read, move, and work with all energy throughout this ecosystem. It's a lot different for them. They can easily ignore the energy that surrounds them, but that doesn't mean that normal is better. Sounds very sexy, but it doesn't mean that it's better.

Do you know what normal actually means? It means conforming to a standard, a usual, typical, or expected standard. You are not normal, my friend. You are extremely, extremely special.

Normal does come with its own unique set of problems, and this is a good way to look at things. Especially sometimes when you start to feel depressed or feel like, "Why does this have to be happening to me?"

Normal people also have to navigate through life differently than you do, and these are things you want to remember when you're wondering, *Why do I have to have this gift?*

1) They tend to struggle a lot more when it comes to the relationships in their life.

This is very common. Empaths can struggle with relationships, but they have a lot more clarity when it comes to the relationships in their life and how they're navigating through those relationships.

2) They have a much harder time being guided by the divine, the universe, or their guides.

Normal people tend to have a much harder time being guided by the divine, the universe, or their guides. Even when they're dealing with the simple task of developing their psychic senses and abilities, they can have a harder time learning how to connect with their spiritual bodies and psychic senses.

They are physical body dominant and earth energy tends to be a dominant frequency with them. The issue with this is you always want to have a balance between your spiritual and physical bodies, not allowing one to be dominant over the other, by encouraging a partnership between the two. Because of this an Empath ability will always give you a bit of an edge when it comes to being guided by the divine, the universe, and your guides.

3) They tend to subject themselves to dangerously high amounts of negativity and toxicity.

Now, just because a normal person has a much easier time ignoring the energy around them, it doesn't mean they're still not experiencing some really strong effects on their physical body. The ignorance is bliss approach can, and absolutely will, affect things like your blood pressure and stress levels, so they can easily subject themselves to high amounts of negativity and toxicity.

The cool thing about being an Empath is you can feel negativity and toxicity affecting your body before it does major damage inside your physical body such as your cardiovascular system, your stomach, or creating illnesses such as chronic fatigue or fibromyalgia.

As an Empath you can learn how to shift those relationships and address negativity and toxicity in your life before it becomes something you just ignore and overlook instead of one day seemingly out of the blue realizing you are having some major health issues.

4) They tend to live their life with higher stress levels.

Because normal people have a strong ability to ignore and overlook things such as high amounts of negativity or toxicity, they tend to live their life with higher stress levels than Empaths.

When you're not so aware of the energy you are surrounding yourself with, including how this impacts your choice making, you can go about making poor choices or doing things that are not conducive to your energetic environment. The typical mindset being, "Oh, it's okay, it's fine, I'm fine. I can push through this. This is just life."

5) They settle...a lot...

An Empath doesn't settle very well, because if you do, you can't ignore that very uncomfortable feeling of *something feels off to me, this feeling is very uncomfortable, I need to fix this.* You want to strive to fix that uncomfortable feeling. This is why Empaths don't tend to settle as much, which is a super cool trait. So thank goodness you are not normal.

It is a wonderful gift to have, but it has to constantly be managed, which can be incredibly exhausting and overwhelming. Some days you're just like, "Why? Why do I have to do this all the time with all the other things I have to do?" But I'm going to really help you out with that. We're going to do some shifting throughout this book and transform the way you live so you don't have to feel so weighed down by this gift.

Nonetheless, the struggle is real because now you have to learn how to manage your gift and learn how to live your life differently. However, it will be a little easier if you keep these simple things in mind.

You are different than other people.

This mind shift and perspective will help you a lot. I know I've covered this a bit already, but I really want to drive this home. Especially because Empaths tend to want to do things the same way their friends are, or their family. Believe me I know, because I wanted to do this myself. And I learned very quickly, you simply can't do that and feel well. You can't follow the crowd; their rules don't apply to you.

You will hang out with people who don't understand your gift, friends and family members.

This is a very normal thing to do. In fact, it should be encouraged. However, it's important to realize you can't explain to someone who doesn't have the gift what it's like to be an Empath. That's like explaining to someone who doesn't have children what it's like to have children. While they might try to understand it as best they can, they just have no frame of reference to what it's actually like. That's through no fault of their own.

For instance, if they want to go to a concert, or to a place where there's a lot of weird energy. If you try explaining to them you will need some time to prepare yourself, or you may need some time to work into it, or even that you don't want to do something because it feels like it will be tough for you, you may get some pushback or feel like they are not empathizing with your situation, which is fair, because they simply do not have a frame of reference for what it's like. You can't fault them for that because they have no idea what you're talking about. They may even think you're making things up or you're being overdramatic.

As an Empath, hopefully you've surrounded yourself with supportive, understanding people. However, you will hang out with the oblivious on occasion; there's just no way around it. Try not to take it personal. Best-case scenario is limiting the amount of information you share with them about your gift to keep from having to defend yourself against something they clearly cannot understand.

You will be jealous of "normal" people on occasion.

Oddly enough, on occasion, you might even find yourself jealous of these same people because you want to go do these things. And you may feel a lot of FOMO (fear of missing out) if you don't do these things. Yet it might just be too much work, or it might feel too overwhelming to do these things.

You will want to pretend as if you are "normal."

When jealousy kicks in, it's common to want to pretend as if you're normal too. I even did this. I was just like, *Okay, I'm tired of this, I'm just going to pretend like it's not a thing and it'll go away*, which is totally normal. You might find yourself thinking, *I'm just going to power through*. *If I just can pretend like I don't have it, then it's not going to be a problem*.

Well, I can tell you when I was young, I tried this many times. I really tried to rid myself of this gift. Clearly that did not work out very well.

But it's not about ridding yourself of this gift and trying to be normal. The key is to learn how to feel better as an Empath with knowledge, acceptance, and consistency.

Lastly, but also very important...

Managing your abilities must be consistent.

This is going to take an entire chapter on its own, so let's get into that next...

CHAPTER 12
Living An Empowered Empath Lifestyle

When it comes to managing your ability, and learning how to feel good, consistency is very, very important...

You need to be committed. If you're only half in, you will only feel a little better, but if you want to become an Empowered Empath, consistency is a must.

It's okay if you mess up once in a while, because believe me, you will mess up and you will notice. The key is going to be how you react.

You will need to be committed to learning about your gift and how to recognize specific habits and patterns you develop over time that are not aligned with living an Empowered Empath lifestyle.

Everybody's a little bit different. Everyone has habits and patterns. Some of these will be habits that you'll need to break if you want to feel good, healthy and empowered.

You might find yourself feeling like, *I'm doing good! I'm getting this all figured out. Everything feels great.* When that happens, just like many things in life, you might start slacking off a little bit. You may forget some of the stuff you were doing, especially when you're in the early stages of managing your gift.

However, this is a transformational journey.

Because it's a transformation journey, you'll slack off, you'll forget about your maintenance, and then you'll start feeling crappy again. You'll find yourself wondering, *Why do I feel this way again? It was going so well. What was I doing differently?* That's when you can backtrack and remember what you were doing, and where things went off the rails, trying to figure out what areas you were slacking in. Why is this bound to happen? Because let's face it, we are still human.

The good news is as you become more familiar with your gift, how your spiritual and physical bodies work with energy, and how it affects you on a personal level, it becomes fairly easy to self-correct. And you can make adjustments pretty quickly.

Becoming an Empowered Empath requires a lifestyle change.

This is where your transformational journey begins to take shape by learning how to live an energetically healthier existence. All the techniques you will learn in this series are meant to work together. They're meant to guide you through this lifestyle change. So don't just pick your favorites. You want to think long-term, such as creating new eating habits versus dieting.

For instance, when you create new eating habits, you must learn how to shop differently, cook differently, and eat out differently. It's essentially the same type of thing. This is why I created a system for this. An Empowered Empath lifestyle is a system I've been working on for 20-plus years. It's how I live my life now, and it's what you're going to learn here. The heart of this system is very basic, very simple, and it's going to involve:

- **E**mpowering your spiritual body
- **M**anaging your abilities
- **P**rotecting your energy
- **A**wareness and action
- **T**raining and development
- **H**ealing others

You're going to learn empowerment of the spiritual body because you will need to learn how to strengthen your energetic system.

You're going to learn how to manage your abilities and manage your energy.

How to protect your energy, as well as awareness and action. And how to become very aware of what's causing you to not feel well.

This will allow you to take action by learning how to shift your energy, or your particular habits with energy.

Then training and development. You will be training and learning how to live this lifestyle and develop your abilities.

Lastly, we'll touch upon healing others because you're going to want to use your healing abilities in a more focused manner if you are drawn towards being a healer.

However, there are a lot of moving parts to this journey, and that's where the training part comes in. It will change many things in your life. Living an Empowered Empath lifestyle and working with this system will change your life for the better. It will change your relationship with everything. For me, it literally transformed how I felt like I was living.

- It will change your relationship with yourself.

- Your relationships with other people.

- Your relationship with money.

- Your relationship with universal energy.

It changed my relationship with so many things. I was so grateful to finally figure out this system. So let's get started with the first part of our transformational journey.

CHAPTER 13
What Happens During an Empath Awakening

Most everyone who is developing spiritually experiences a spiritual awakening of some kind. *Think of it more like an experience than an actual event.*

On a spiritual journey you are guided towards new places that feel somewhat familiar to you. At each new place you experience another layer to your spiritual awakening, and if you're lucky, this will last a lifetime...

An Empath Awakening is a little bit different. *It can be a bit more intense than normal.*

With a spiritual awakening, it's easier to navigate throughout your journey; you can ignore things you don't want to see, move at your own pace, and stop once in a while for a rest.

An Empath awakening is connected to your Empath abilities, and more often than not these abilities can and will pick up momentum all on their own. Once it starts, it's hard to stop...

That would be kind of like trying to stop a flower from blooming or a tree from growing.

Imagine a rose, one which hasn't blossomed yet. Each petal is layered very closely together to form the bud of the flower. When you are very grounded in your physical body, the same thing occurs: you are heavily layered with physical energy.

Each layer creates a "buffer" of energy that keeps your spiritual body essentially cocooned. When nature decides it's time, the layers will begin to peel back, and blooming begins.

An Empath awakening happens when your spiritual body has played a dormant role for many years, allowing the physical body to become primary. When your spiritual body takes a back seat role, your primary focus becomes all things physical. Your physical body, your physical senses, fear, and logic, and you live your life accordingly.

In a world where your physical body is primary, things such as material items, status, and making the best money possible are very important to you. You feel akin to your neighbors, family, and friends as they are also on the same journey.

Until one day, your spiritual body begins to awaken. Like a rose, when nature decides it's time, the layers will begin to peel back, and that's when the blooming begins.

Imagine it like a flower that's been closed at night, dormant. Then in the morning it gets proper water and sunlight and decides it's time to blossom. It turns towards the sunlight, and the petals begin to open. It's beautiful.

Well, it's morning now, after a very long night that's lasted most of your life. The frequency of the earth is shifting, raising its vibrational frequency to a much higher frequency, one that's more aligned with the spiritual realm where the sun is shining.

And you can feel it. You can feel something stirring deep within your soul. You can feel your vibration wanting to turn towards the sun, it's craving spiritual energy, and it wants to blossom.

The blooming is just the beginning. When the blooming starts, an Empath awakening begins. Each time you peel back a layer, you connect more and more with your spiritual body and your spiritual self, and you begin to rediscover yourself from your soul's point of view. And this is when you essentially begin looking at your life with a whole new set of eyes. Your spiritual eyes open, and things look different. It can feel like you've needed glasses for years, and you've just put them on for the very first time...and you can see.

You have a much clearer picture, a different perspective from a spiritual point of view. As you peel back the layers, not only do you gain some clarity, *this is where you start empowering your spiritual body and forming a strong bond between your spiritual and physical bodies.*

You start to tune in with how you're feeling on a spiritual level while acknowledging it on a physical level. This is where some really productive work begins.

There are essentially seven different stages of an Empath awakening. But it's important to remember these four things...

1) An Empath awakening is different from a spiritual awakening.

It's more intense. With a spiritual awakening, it's easier to navigate through your journey because you can ignore things you don't want to see, and you can move at your own pace. You can even stop and be like, *I don't want to do this right now, so I'm just going to chill on the spiritual stuff for a little bit.*

An Empath awakening is connected to your Empath abilities. The difference is these abilities can and will pick up momentum all on their own. And once this process starts, it is hard to stop.

2) Every person will go through these stages differently.

You might blaze through certain stages and have a harder time with others. An Empath awakening is really a unique awakening process.

3) It will be your own personal experience.

Everyone's awakening is different. If you talk to somebody about it, talk to friends, family, or other Empaths about your experience, keep in mind that everybody will have their own unique personal experience.

4) How long you're in each stage is not important.

If you're blazing through some of the stages but not others it's fine, it's not a contest. How long you're staying in each stage is irrelevant. What is important is learning how to empower your spiritual body.

You may have spent your whole life living a very physical lifestyle, allowing your physical body to be primarily dominant. You've made choices, gathered friends, and created a lifestyle that all revolves around this system. A system that works hard to dismiss anything involving the spiritual realm.

The problem with this is you are both spiritual and physical, so this is not conducive to living a healthy life as a spiritual being in a physical body.

And here's something that's even more interesting.

Your physical body actually receives information on how to operate from your spiritual body and its frequency.

How to feel, how to react, and how to heal.

When you get your signals crossed, and ignore your spiritual body and its frequency, things don't go very well. Your own interference can cause disruption in a very functional system.

Which leads us to our next section, *Seven Different Stages of An Empath Awakening.*

Part Two

**Section 2
Seven Different Stages of An Empath Awakening**

CHAPTER 14

Stage 1 – Spiritual Crisis

L et's talk about stage one, which is a Spiritual Crisis. When you're peeling back the first layer, when you're starting to bloom, *many Empaths will experience frustration.*

And it can literally feel like it comes out of nowhere.

Your life might feel like it's going just fine. Then all of a sudden, things change. You might feel:

- Frustrated with your job.

- Frustrated with your relationship, or several relationships.

- Feeling unsettled with where you're at in life.

- Feeling more irritated than normal.

But you can't quite put your finger on what's happening. So where is this all coming from?

This is what's called a spiritual crisis.

A spiritual crisis is where Empaths first start experiencing some type of discord within their spiritual bodies.

And since it's normal human behavior to point fingers outside of ourselves, naturally you might find yourself thinking things like:

It must be my job.
It's definitely where I live.
It's got to be my boss.
It's my significant other.
My kids are making me crazy.
My family is driving me nuts.

When you don't understand how it feels to be out of alignment with your spiritual body, it can be very confusing. So how do you get out of alignment?

By doing things that don't align with your spiritual happiness. It's easy to make decisions from a physical point of view when you can't feel your spiritual body and when your spiritual body is buffered with energy. People tend to make decisions based upon:

- Fear and worry
- Pleasing other people.
- Filling a void temporarily with physical "stuff."

It's what people do, and you learn from example. It just seems normal.

It's how most everyone grows up, and most likely you're surrounded by people who are also doing this very same thing. Since you've been taught how to do this from a very young age, most of your friends, family members, parents, and everybody who encompasses your life are probably doing this too.

However, change is inevitable, and it needs to happen to start the empowerment process.

The point of experiencing a spiritual crisis is to **_learn what truly makes you happy at the core of your soul_**. And I'm going to give you a hint. This is not going to involve money. It's not going to involve a car or house or anything physical. This type of thinking is based upon a physical point of view mindset.

It will, however, involve things such as *time, freedom, love, travel, and life experiences.*

When you're having an Empath awakening and you're learning how to work with universal energy. You need to retrain your brain on how to start working with this powerful energy from a spiritual point of view mindset. A spiritual point of view does not have dollars or coins attached to it. It revolves around the energy of time, the energy of freedom, and the energy of life experiences.

But to do that, you will need to figure out what your soul desires truly are. Most likely up until this point, especially if you're in the spiritual crisis stage, you might have been thinking everything was fine. You were happy and things were going well. You had the kids, the car, and the house or whatever that picture looked like for you.

If this sounds like you, you've probably been primarily living a dominant physical body lifestyle. Heavily buffered physical energy, because those things all revolve around physical energy.

Physically Dominant + Physical Mindset = Physical Desires

However, once you find yourself starting the process of an Empath awakening, you're going to find out that on a soul level, these things are very unsatisfactory. And this is where a lot of frustration enters the picture, and the spiritual crisis stage sets in.

This stage can feel super unstable and very nerve-wracking to your foundation because you've been going about life all these years thinking you knew what made you happy.

Then suddenly, there is this earthquake of energy that you start continuously experiencing, and it's shaking things up for you.

Which is confusing as you look around and think, *Wow, my foundation of happiness is not what I thought it was. I'm feeling lost and confused about what that even means to me anymore.* You find yourself feeling like you are in the midst of a mid-life crisis on a spiritual level.

To start the empowerment process, you need to start putting some deep thought into these questions.

1. What do you desire most in life?
2. What are you doing to fulfill your spiritual self?
3. Do you feel happy?
4. How often do you feel happy?
5. Do you feel as if you are aligned or have a purpose?
6. What choices are you making to move towards alignment?
7. Are you breaking or repeating patterns?

When you're starting the empowerment process, you need to learn how to get in tune with what makes your soul happy and thrive because that's how you connect in and begin working with a higher vibrational frequency.

And it's from this place, working with a higher vibrational frequency, that you can really shift things in your life. You have access to a powerful spiritual guidance system, Universal Laws, and fulfillment on a level that is deep within your soul.

Before a Spiritual Crisis stage, it's quite easy to go through life stuffing down any feelings that might question your current path and decision making, because they feel like discord, so you put a cork in it to keep it at bay. You dismiss it by reassuring yourself:

It doesn't really matter what makes me happy because I'm already in this situation.

This is how I set my life up.

This is what I'm supposed to do.

This is how I pay my bills.

This is how I navigate through life.

It's my existence right now.

But that isn't how it has to be, or even how it's supposed to be. Especially when you learn how to really **work with** universal energy, and you learn how to **work with** your Empath abilities. In fact, change is inevitable, whether you're on board with it or not.

Let's talk about alignment for a minute.

My guess is since you are reading this book, you're probably not feeling aligned, or as aligned as you should feel at this very moment in time. Which means you're probably feeling some sort of discord sign somewhere. So how can you tell if your alignment is off?

You can start by asking yourself some of these questions...

- Does everything feel as if things are lining up for me like dominoes?

- Does it feel like the energy in my life is fluid and flowing nicely and easily?

- Are things going well for me? (And don't worry if they're not, because this is what we are working on.)

- Am I currently making choices to help me move towards better alignment?

Reading this book might be one of them. It might be one of your first steps towards moving to better alignment.

If you're not feeling aligned right now, if your answer to any of these questions is no (besides the last one), then I feel you've been incredibly honest with yourself. And that can be really hard to do. Self-awareness is a huge part of this process.

This means there will be some changes that you're going to need to implement. And you can start by asking yourself, **What choices am I currently making to move towards better alignment?**

Self-awareness is so important. You need to become more fully aware of your daily, weekly, and monthly choices. If you can't think of any, now's a good time to brainstorm on what choices you could make that might help fulfill yourself on a spiritual level better moving forward. Think of it like planting seeds for the future.

They're usually pretty simple things, so try not to make this a Mt. Everest moment, and make it feel too overwhelming. Your perspective is important here. **Don't worry so much about "the how" and focus more on the outcome.** Just pretend like the how is just going to work out for you. This is really, really important.

Next you will want to ask yourself, **are you starting to break patterns, or do you feel like you're repeating**

them? Most likely, if you're not quite implementing change yet and making different choices than you have in the past, ***you're repeating patterns.***

If your life has been the same for the last few years, it's definitely a sign that you are on a repetitive path.

Which makes this a good thing to give some thought to, especially because we're going to spend some time breaking old patterns. I want you to feel well and I want you to feel healthy, and you will have to break old patterns to do that, just like I did. I really had to break through a certain mindset and perspective and bust through some old patterns that continued to repeat themselves because they became a habit.

Commitment is also very important at this stage. Especially because most likely ***it will take some time to familiarize yourself with the desires you've lost touch with.*** This will help you figure out how to get to the root of your happiness, and only then can you begin to implement changes.

You need to know what your goal is. You need a destination and a goal to properly and effectively implement changes and pave a new road. If you just start repaving your old road without a destination, that's not going to be very helpful.

This brings us to stage two, Spiritual Depression.

CHAPTER 15

Stage 2 – Spiritual Depression

Stage two of an Empath awakening is called Spiritual Depression.

Depression can have a heavy stigma attached to it or a heavy weight, and I want you to throw those perceptions out the window, because there's also some very cool stuff that can happen during this stage. And you need to experience these things, to be able to transform your life as an Empath, so this is a good stage to go through, even though it sounds really horrible.

In stage one, many times as an Empath you will feel like you have been living life in a way that felt pretty good for many years. Then, seemingly out of nowhere, you begin to experience a Spiritual Crisis, which can be pretty jolting on a soul level, leaving you feeling sad, upset, frustrated, and not feeling your best.

And this is when Spiritual Depression can set in. Before you get too concerned, **Spiritual Depression can happen in many different degrees.**

- **Minor** – *Feeling unsettled, lost, and a little sad on occasion.* But this feeling comes and goes in waves.

You are ready to make some shifts. When you are experiencing Spiritual Depression to a minor degree, it's easy to ignore. You might know you need to make some shifts, but the urgency is less.

- **Major** – *Feeling very unhappy with your life.* This feeling can be pretty settled in, but you can still enjoy life on occasion when you shift your focus.

You need to make some changes for the sake of your health and happiness. Most Empaths who are experiencing an awakening tend to fall into this category and your spiritual body is reacting accordingly. It's trying to get your attention as you probably did a good job of dismissing things when you first started feeling unsettled and lost.

- **Extreme** – *Extreme unhappiness and depression.* This feeling makes it hard to enjoy your life. This is usually coupled with heavy anxiety.

You need to make extreme changes. If you ignore these signs for a really long period of time, you'll end up gradually moving into the extreme stage. If you still dismiss the signs and signals, it will continue to grow momentum until you can no longer ignore what's happening.

As far as anxiety goes, Empaths are very prone to anxiety because of their natural ability to feel and read energy. If you're not managing your energy properly, you can have anxiety no matter where you're landing on this scale. You can experience it with any of these categories.

Now, stage one Spiritual Crisis, and stage two Spiritual Depression are really closely related. When you no longer have the ability to ignore your spiritual body, which is basically what happens when you start to experience an Empath awakening, this is when you discover something kind of alarming.

What you thought made you happy and aligned with your happiness, actually aligned with the physical world and not the spiritual world.

In other words, it brought you physical happiness, not spiritual happiness...

Spiritual happiness is when you are fulfilled and satisfied on a spiritual level and your soul feels healthy. And this is achieved when you accomplish these three things:

- You learn how to align both your spiritual and physical bodies.

- You are aligned with your purpose, or you are aware of and actively pursuing your purpose.

- You've learned how to raise your vibration and maintain a higher spiritual frequency level.

During a Spiritual Depression stage is usually when an Empath becomes very aware of their spiritual happiness, it becomes a factor. But it's also where things start to get kind of cool. This stage tends to be very reminiscent for some people, for very specific reasons...

Children are very, very aware of their spiritual happiness. It's super important to them. Children always, always naturally gravitate towards what brings them joy at that moment in time.

And it never has anything to do with a new car or a bigger house because it's typically not money related. They are using their creativity, they're laughing, they're bonding with you, they're experiencing new things in nature. Life experience is very important to them.

Their happiness doesn't typically revolve around physical items unless you've walked them in that direction, where they focus on getting a new toy or something. This can happen, but for the most part, even if you buy them the new toy, after a while, it will be discarded. Then they want to run around and play chase or play with their friends or gravitate towards another fun life experience.

The younger you are, the more aligned you are with your spiritual body and therefore more aware of your spiritual happiness.

In the later teen years, there's a little bit more weight that becomes a factor because of parents and teachers, and the pressures put on you to become successful. This is where things take a turn. This is usually when money enters the picture. Older teens are **expected** to move away from their spiritual happiness because it won't make them money; that's not responsible.

How are you going to support yourself?

What kind of decisions are you going to make in life?

What career are you going to choose?

You are expected to set yourself up well and have a good solid path that makes sense to the other people around you and makes **them** feel comfortable. When it comes to following your passion or your dreams, you better do something that has a solid track record.

People who surround older teens often view creativity as a waste of time and not something they would promote or be on board with, because taking an unknown path, or taking a chance on your passion? Well, that would be out-of-the-box thinking, and a lot of people don't think that way. That's scary for adults, who certainly don't want to work through their own fears about doing something like that.

You are taught to ignore your spiritual body as you grow up. And the older you get, the easier it becomes.

Especially when you start doing adulting things, like having to pay rent, get married, have kids, a career, and all the other adult things you are "required" to do.

What if things had been different for you growing up?

What if every career choice or opportunity paid the same amount of money in life?

What if you could choose to be anything you wanted in life and be able to support yourself?

Wouldn't that be amazing? Can you imagine the possibilities? The happiness? The alignment? There would be no need to go off track and circle back years later trying to find that place. That place of happiness...*only if happiness was promoted in the first place as a priority when choosing your path.*

When you become more spiritually aware, you naturally feel the urge to circle back and see where you took a wrong turn in the first place.

Circling back is where many adults are now.

After years of ignoring your spiritual body and trying to find happiness through money and acceptance, that's when you find out happiness was not at the end of that physical path.

It's here that you begin the realignment process; circling back involves going back to a time in your life when you felt the most aligned. It's smart and it's natural.

The issue with this is it can actually make any feelings of discord even stronger, which contributes to Spiritual Depression. Instead of using that information to rediscover your joys, talents, and who you are on a spiritual level, *people can tend to hang out in the past with regrets.* This is why it's so important to be aware of this pitfall so you can avoid it.

Circling back should be used as part of *an awareness process, or a place of knowledge.* Super good information lies in your past if you use it to your advantage and not as a detriment. Then it becomes a part of your empowerment process.

Stage two is a very beneficial stage when learning how to *empower your spiritual body.* When you reconnect with a more aligned you (past), while you are in a spiritual crisis (present), your spiritual memory begins to kick in.

Your spiritual memory holds very important knowledge on how to achieve alignment with your spiritual body.

Searching your memories for a time in your life when you were younger and when you may have felt like you followed joy, and you were just purely happy. Doing regular things such as being in nature or being with people. This is powerful information that is very beneficial when it comes to learning how to empower your spiritual body—allowing you to reconnect with a more aligned version of yourself, which is huge.

Your spiritual memory is also where the good stuff is.

And stage two is usually where this is triggered. It's like a spiritual road map. It's where all the valuable information is on how it "feels" to be aligned.

Here's a good exercise to try:

Reach back into your life to find the last time you remember being aligned by "reminiscing."

When was the last time you remember really, truly being happy? Not just a day, but a timeframe, for many days or months at a time.

When did you feel lighter? Lighter than you do today.

When did it feel like things flowed more easily?

When was the last time you remember feeling carefree? Little to no worries? Or even when you did worry feeling confident things would work out okay?

When was the last time you felt secure?

When was the last time you felt less pressure on yourself?

This process will trigger a "spiritual memory" on how it felt to be aligned.

When you go back and find that place in your life, it feels really good. Your spiritual memory kicks in and you remember...

Yes, I remember this feeling.

I felt so good.

I was so light.

I felt like everything just flowed so nicely.

I felt a lot more joy and happiness in my life.

That's when it's important to follow that memory to the "root of your alignment." How you made spiritual happiness a priority, and everything else fell into place.

This exercise is designed to give you a *frame of reference*, not to give you a place to hang out. We are not supposed to be **aligning** with old memories, we are **exploring** them. The reason some Empaths get stuck in their past is instead of using that knowledge to **shift** their current position moving forward, they try to **recreate** that part of their past.

Through this process, you will experience the good, the bad, and the ugly.

Let's start with the ugly...

When you are experiencing discord, connecting with how you felt when you were a younger, "more aligned" version of yourself, in some instances it can lead to more confusion.

This is where you might feel the urge to recreate parts of your old life. The thought process being, "I was happier when I..."

- Lived there.

- Had a relationship with so and so.

- Worked there.

- Was doing XYZ.

And the brain goes, let's make that happen! What the brain skips over is it wasn't the place or the people that made you feel aligned and happier.

When you follow a spiritual memory to the root of your alignment, where you were the happiest and things were falling into place nicely, this is where you want to go, but you don't want to recreate that version of your life again. You're not trying to recreate where you lived. You're not trying to recreate your career. You're not trying to recreate a relationship. It simply will not work. The past is the past for a reason, and you are not the same person you were then...emotionally, vibrationally, or physically.

Instead, you want to tune into a different aspect of how you were living your life at the time and ask yourself these questions:

- How was I making better choices than I am now?

- How were my circumstances different?

- What was my focus?

- What was my mindset? My perspective?

- Was I more carefree?

- How was my confidence then?

- What was my relationship with my spiritual senses?

- What was my relationship with source energy? God, angels, spirit guides?

Most likely, you were not making choices based on *fear and worry*.

Next, we will talk about the bad...

As I mentioned it wasn't the place, or the people, that made you feel aligned and happier. *It was how you were living your life at the time.*
The bad news is this can take a while to discover.

Here's the good news...

By remembering the last time you felt spiritually aligned, you can actually figure out where you started to run off the rails in the first place. You can actually retrace your alignment!
Which is super helpful information. Since you were born in alignment, at some point in time, you learned how to "shift" your focus from spiritual happiness to physical happiness. This is where your course began to take a very different turn.

How did things begin to go so wrong? I blame fear.

Fear and doubt are taught and trained behaviors handed down through generations. It is something you are exposed to at a very young age. Not just through families, but through society as well.
At first, you're immune to it, and you brush it off because you don't see fear the same way other people do when you're younger. It's not a primary focus. You think that everybody's being a little bit overzealous about this fear thing.

But after a while, as you get older, these low-vibration emotions can really wear you down, and energetically it just becomes too much weight.

You start being bombarded with it everywhere. You watch things happen to all these fearful people who manifested life experiences from a place of fear-based thinking. Then it starts to feel like your reality, especially for an Empath, since you can feel and sense fear in others around you as you get older. Parents, teachers, grandparents, even friends, all seem fearful or worrisome about life.

When the energy around you becomes too heavy, as an Empath this when you begin the process of ***unplugging from your spiritual body.***

If you're not taught otherwise, you will naturally go into self-preservation mode. If you don't go into self-preservation mode and shut your gift down, your Empath gift will continue to blossom. However, unplugging is the only way most Empaths learn how to navigate feeling energetic weight that feels so heavy and uncomfortable. It's the only way you know how to preserve your own energy.

When you unplug and disconnect from your spiritual senses, your spiritual frequency lowers.

And when that happens, you lose some very important knowledge.

You will begin to lose your ability to differentiate your own feelings from others.

When you unplug, you essentially disconnect from the root of where your Empath abilities stem from, ***which creates spiritual fog***

Spiritual fog is just like it sounds; it makes it harder to gain clarity when trying to use your spiritual senses. When you lose the ability to differentiate your feelings from others, you've become a mirror without knowledge.

What happens if you're a mirror, but you don't know you're a mirror? You begin the process of taking on other people's emotions including fear, doubt, and worry. ***Their emotions become part of your own life experience.***

How do you get back on track?

It's called the Empath Circle of Life... To become a healthy Empath, you need to understand how an Empath Circle of Life works.

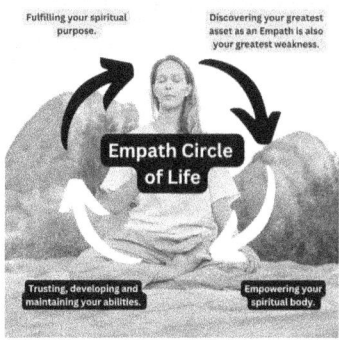

1) Discovering your greatest asset as an Empath is also your greatest weakness.

As an Empath, you're a natural healer and a natural nurturer. You want to help heal and nurture everybody around you, but being able to do both things to the best of your ability does not mean self-sacrifice.

As an Empath, self-sacrifice is something you most likely do, and do very well. Your priorities lie with the care and healing of other people while not considering the consequences of your actions. *This actually weakens your ability to use your gift optimally...*

2) Empowering your spiritual body.

If you truly want to help heal others to the best of your ability, it is imperative to really learn how to build a solid foundation with your spiritual body. You may want to move on to helping others right away because it feels good. You feel satisfied in the moment, but you will suffer the after-effects of an unstable foundation, including weakness, dizziness, fatigue, anger, and irritability. It affects your overall well-being and your health.

3) Trusting, developing and maintaining your abilities.

With special emphasis on maintenance. Trusting and development are the easiest part. It's the maintenance that becomes an issue. Maintaining your Empath abilities means learning how to use your abilities properly with your spiritual and physical bodies. It means not allowing your two bodies to break down as a consequence of your actions.

4) Fulfilling your spiritual purpose.

As an Empath, you're a healer, but how this works with your spiritual purpose can take on all kinds of shapes. But truly empowering yourself is the only way you will be able to fulfill your spiritual purpose. Healing can be done in so many different ways it would make your head spin. But here's something you might not know. You have several purposes throughout your lifetime, not just one.

Which brings us to stage three, Spiritual Purpose.

CHAPTER 16

Stage 3 – Spiritual Purpose

I absolutely love this stage because this is when you really start to take some control over empowering your spiritual body.

It's where you begin to take action.

When you're in stage one or stage two, you're feeling a little bit off your foundation. You feel nervous and unsure about what's happening. You know that there are changes taking place, but nothing feels stable. It can be a little worrisome. When you go through those stages and start sorting through what's working for you and what's not, it creates a different perspective, and therefore a different connection with your spiritual body, and it's where you begin to take action.

When you're searching for your purpose, desire becomes strong, and action will begin to take over. You might start by simply doing research on some things you might find interesting, such as new job opportunities, and taking some new classes to see what resonates with you.

Or you might be more aggressive with your pursuits by implementing changes right away. Maybe you think:

I've always wanted to go to Europe, I'm not getting any younger, I'm just going to go!

I've always wanted to live here. You know what? I'm going to move!

Or XYZ feels good to me. So I'm going to head that direction.

Even if you don't know what your purpose is, the fact that you're actively looking is really going to change a lot for you.

This is where you begin your first stages of spiritual alignment. And it's going to bring some really cool stuff into your life...

It's going to bring knowledge.

It's going to bring signs, signals, and synchronicities.

Did you know that one of the first signs of spiritual alignment is becoming more aware of coincidences than ever before? Ones that you would have normally overlooked.

- **Spiritual Messages** ~ Such as seeing feathers, coins, birds, etc. are typically signs related to spirits, angels, or loved ones. You wouldn't be able to receive that message or even have the awareness of a spiritual message if you weren't starting to become aligned.

- **Synchronistic or Repetitive Number Sequences** ~ Are something you might also begin to take notice of, which are also spiritual messages and signs of alignment.

- **Intuitive Hits** ~ Such as I am feeling like I should or shouldn't go this direction. Intuitive hits could involve physical signs or visual ones, synchronicities, or that you are noticing within the body.

- **Telepathic Connections** ~ Such as thinking about somebody and they called, or you have a feeling you need to call them.

These are examples and signs that you're beginning the first stages of spiritual alignment.

Becoming more aligned as an Empath also means getting rid of energetic junk.

Everything is not always going to align perfectly, or even work well during this stage. And that's okay because this is where you learn how to sort out heavy energy, or the junk.

You learn to compartmentalize and how to sort through things that align or do not align with your spiritual body.

It's when you become more familiar with your true self and begin creating a relationship with your spiritual body, the body that moves with you through many, many lifetimes. This is when you really start creating that bond and solidifying the relationship between both your spiritual and physical bodies. ***And this is incredibly, incredibly powerful!***

However, to find your purpose, you must first find spiritual happiness.

Your purpose and your spiritual happiness are very closely linked and intertwined. They go hand in hand.

- Your spiritual body and spiritual empowerment are directly linked to your spiritual happiness.

- Your spiritual happiness is directly linked to achieving and maintaining a higher vibrational or spiritual frequency.

- A higher frequency is directly linked to bringing about spiritual clarity.

- Spiritual clarity allows you to connect with your spiritual purpose.

Discovering what makes you happy can be a little more complex than you might have thought. You need to know what it is you are looking for, and where your focus should be. There are basically two types of happiness.

1) Physical happiness.

This is when you desire and acquire physical things. This type of happiness is linked to your physical body.

2) Spiritual happiness.

This is when you desire deeper fulfillment, on a spiritual level. This type of happiness is linked to your spiritual body.

One is not necessarily better than the other, because everyone needs some of both in their life. *It's more about finding a balance between your two bodies.*

Because of things you hear, you might be under the impression that if you develop your spiritual senses and you're very aligned on a spiritual level, physical desires should no longer be important to you. Those desires should be a thing of the past. You should be very satisfied with everything on a soul level. Well, that's not true because we are still human, and we are physical beings that live in a physical world. It's important to have both things in your life, some physical happiness and some spiritual happiness.

Let's talk about physical happiness first...

When you are experiencing physical happiness, you are experiencing things with your physical senses, and this can be quite enjoyable!

- ***Let's start with physically seeing.*** There are all different types of things you can experience with seeing that can bring you physical joy or happiness. Seeing physical beauty such as art, a sunset, nature, people, or animals..

- ***Next let's talk about physical touch.*** Physical touch between two people, such as a hug or intimacy, or even animals such as a pet.

- ***Then there's physically hearing.*** Such as listening to music or a loved one's voice. Listening to nature such as the trees, birds, the rain, or the ocean.

- ***Lastly there is physically smelling.*** Such as smelling food, pastries, or flowers

All these things can be very powerful physical experiences. That in turn brings about physical happiness.

But there are three important things that you need to know...

1) Physical happiness is the easiest to achieve.

It doesn't take much to buy physical items or experience things with your physical senses.

2) It's something you are most likely very well acquainted with.

Most likely you are already very acquainted with your desires on a physical level. This is something you've spent most of your life becoming acquainted with.

3) Physical happiness is very temporary.

It never lasts very long unless it's in combination with experiencing spiritual happiness at the same time.

You shouldn't feel guilty about having physical desires. In fact, experiencing physical happiness is important to experience as well. It is a part of your physical experience.

Now let's talk about spiritual happiness...

This is where things get a bit more difficult. When you experience spiritual happiness you experience it with your spiritual senses, and this can be quite satisfying on a soul level.

- ***Experiencing spiritual beauty.*** Such as commitment, love, or a bond.

- *Touching another person vibrationally.* Such as love or healing.

- *Feeling universal energy.* Flow, abundance, space, or time.

- *Connecting with spiritual energy.* Guidance, your intuition, desires, purpose, or source...

When you experience things with your spiritual senses, it triggers a powerful response in your spiritual body.

Learning how to shift the focus of your happiness, existence, and life away primarily from the physical, and learning to shift your focus more towards your spiritual body to bring about a better balance can be very confusing, especially for Empaths.

This is why I've put together some fundamentals for you to help find your purpose, take action, and pursue things of interest to you.

Five Fundamentals to Finding Your Purpose:

1) Action – Taking action and pursuing things of interest to you, being curious, searching for opportunity. This helps move your compass towards spiritual alignment.

2) Alignment – When you begin the process of taking action, spiritual happiness becomes a primary focus, which means you now have a destination. This destination requires a journey. This journey will entail learning (by trial and error) what makes you spiritually happy, and what makes you physically happy. This helps you sort out the energetic junk.

3) Clarity – Sorting out the energetic junk (old beliefs, social media, following the crowd, listening to others trying to point you in the *direction of their happiness*) will help bring clarity. Your destination should have one focus in mind—your happiness. This destination can only be navigated by you, because you are the only one who knows the coordinates. It might take some time to uncover, but you hold this information. This is where you start to reconnect with things *you* are passionate about.

4) Passion – Passion points you in the direction of your purpose. You are spiritually gifted in the areas of life you are the most passionate about. Even if you don't feel gifted, you can learn to uncover your spiritual purpose here.

5) Purpose – Your spiritual purpose is deeply intertwined with your spiritual body. This is where spiritual fulfillment happens.

Women tend to put themselves on the back burner when it comes to things they truly enjoy. Men can do this too, but women more often find themselves very intertwined with their husbands and kids. Their family is a primary focus, so they push this aspect of their life away until they're older, when the kids are out of the house doing something on their own, or they find themselves with more time on their hands. This is usually when they notice a void.

You might also feel focusing on yourself is self-indulgent, when it's really about being spiritually healthy. It's about making sure you're maintaining a good balance and promoting good spiritual health. So you need to make sure you shift your mindset and ask yourself...*How healthy do I want to be?*

Each Empath stage is about building upon the other, creating a solid, powerful foundation for you and your spiritual body.

You're creating a connection between your two bodies that doesn't feel weak, but powerful and strong. One that's reliable that you can use often.

Your spiritual purpose is a powerful stepping stone.

Imagine having a bridge that joins two pieces of land together. You can build a bridge with wood planks and rope, allowing it to sway with the weather. This type of bridge can feel unstable and unreliable.

Or you can take your time and put some thought into the purpose and longevity of the bridge. Creating one with a solid foundation, using more stable materials, such as concrete or steel. One that's reliable and strong.

This brings us to our next building block, stage four Spiritual Awareness!

CHAPTER 17

Stage 4 – Spiritual Awareness

After you've been working through trying to find your purpose and what really makes you happy (stage three) you sort of slip into stage four, which is Spiritual Awareness.

- *You start to become more aware of the energies which surround you everywhere.* This is when a lot of people will discover their Empath skills and sensitivities.

- *You begin tuning into your spiritual body more, noticing more things that affect you energetically.* This is when you find you are more sensitive to people, places, and/or things.

- *This will also be the stage where you'll be feeling more drawn to natural things.* You'll be more drawn to natural medicine such as acupuncture and herbs. As well as natural foods.

During this stage there will be *three types of energy* that will require the most attention from you.

While there are many different types of energy, these are going to be the ones tugging on you the most, like a little kid demanding your attention.

1) Live Energy – This is energy generated by people.

2) Earth Energy – This is energy generated through the earth, including things such as plants, foods, herbs, trees, etc.

3) Universal Energy – This is energy generated from the universe surrounding the earth, such as other planets, moons, stars, and even planetary alignment.

Let's talk about live energy for a minute. When you hit stage four and beyond, this will probably be the aha moment for you. Because it's when you really start becoming aware of how "live" energy affects you. Especially when it comes to negative energy.

As an Empath, negativity can and will begin to affect you on a physical level if you're not careful.

In the same way chemicals can be toxic to your physical body, negative energy can be very toxic to the energetic body of an Empath. What's important here is understanding there's a link between your spiritual health and your physical health. They are tied together as one. When you're allowing yourself to be subjected to toxic energy, it will break down the spiritual body.

Because of the close relationship between the two bodies, there is a domino effect that occurs.

Your spiritual body essentially dictates the health of your physical body.

When your energetic (spiritual) body is overexposed to negativity and negative energy, the first thing that is triggered is an emotional response, such as feeling upset, distraught, sad, angry, or hurt.

Emotional responses live within the emotional body, which is directly linked to your spiritual body.

Low vibration emotions and negative responses cause discord within the spiritual body.

If energetic discord is ignored for too long, the physical body will respond. This is what gets your attention. It starts lightly and gains momentum.

Major and minor illnesses are linked to energetic discord. And most everyone is really good at ignoring discord. They think:

I can handle it.
It's just stress, everyone is stressed.
It's just unhappiness, everyone is unhappy.
I can get over it. That's what I'm supposed to do.

What you are essentially saying is everyone else is living in discord, so I will too. But physical health issues stem from your spiritual body. The spiritual body is where all the information on how the physical body works and even heals is stored. And with all the emotional hoarding Empaths do, they can be greatly affected by energetic discord...

Empaths hoard a lot of emotions.

Unintentionally, because you may not realize that it causes so much discord within the body. Because of the way society works, and the things we are taught, people tend to think that if they hoard their emotions, especially if you are an Empath, somehow, you're going to figure out a way to help heal others. If you can just sort through those emotions long enough.

So you don't want to let them go. You really want to work through them:

> You want to think about them.
> Process them.
> Think about them.
> Process them.
> Worry about them.
> Process them.

While under the impression that if we do this long enough, somehow, we will iron out the issue and the energy about the situation will feel better. But obsessing about something that makes you feel a negative response or low vibration emotion does not help remove it or resolve it in any way.

All it does is keep a low-frequency vibration active within your emotional body.

Instead of working through this feeling, what you end up doing is hoarding that feeling within the body. You store it somewhere, even if you don't mean to.

When you hoard energy, you stop the flow of energy, and energy is meant to FLOW...

And this is really important for you to get. When energy becomes stagnant or blocked, especially within any of your bodies, it hinders our ability to carry away old, toxic, or negative energy, which then interferes with our ability to revive and recharge our frequency, and our ability to bring new energy to the space or environment in which it occupies. Not only will this affect your environment, but also your mental, spiritual, and physical health.

You can go to the doctor, and you can learn how to treat symptoms, but in the long run, that's not helpful. I discovered just how valuable this knowledge really is years ago when I was a very young Empath, and I wasn't feeling well.

I was certain there was something physically wrong with me, not knowing that the things I was experiencing were not stemming from my physical body, but **the root of the issue lay within my spiritual body,** which was amplified by the energy I was surrounding and subjecting myself to. It took years before I finally stumbled upon the best discovery ever. One day something clicked, and everything became very apparent...

It was all about energy...and this issue had everything to do with my abilities.

My abilities were affecting my body. I wanted to know how it was affecting my body and why. It became very clear. As an Empath, you have the ability to store a lot of emotions within your emotional and spiritual body, and if you don't learn how to release them and let them go, what occurs next is a natural chain of events.

Your spiritual wellness and mental health will be affected first, and if you continue down the same path, your physical body will then react. It's a natural system response.

This is why it's so important to learn what's serving you and what's not serving you emotionally (which also means spiritually) from a wellness standpoint. And for the things that are not contributing to your spiritual health and wellness, learning how to release that energy and get rid of it is absolutely and unequivocally necessary. So how do you do that?

First, it's awareness.
Then it's learning.
Lastly, it's training.

It's wanting to feel better. It's wanting to feel healthier and more empowered. It's wanting to rid yourself of that energy and then learning how not to repeat the pattern.

Do understand, however, it's not all about negative energy.

Overexposure to live energy in general can also have physical effects, even if it's not negative. Too much exposure causes overload. This is when you can experience:

- Feeling physically drained.
- Feeling tired.
- Feeling anxious.
- Feeling shaky.
- Even feeling out-of-body.

When dealing with live energy it's all about moderation, awareness, and maintenance.

What type of energy are you surrounding yourself with?

Are you hoarding that energy?

Are you holding it in your energetic body?

Anything that you are emotionally dealing with is stuck and held in your energetic or emotional body. It will stay there until you release it.

If you're feeling guilty about something, it's in there.

If you're feeling depressed or sad about something, it's in there.

If you're feeling fearful or worried, it's in there.

Awareness and honesty are really important when it comes to understanding what it is you're holding in your emotional body. You must then learn techniques to help you let go of this low-frequency energy and to trust the higher-frequency energy that you're going to be working with as an Empath. You must trust that you have more control than you realize. And with the right knowledge and mindset, and by cultivating a different relationship with energy, things will always work out for you.

You're going to learn that you don't need to hold on to all this stuff. It's energetic junk, it's garbage, it's what you want to rid yourself of because it's not serving you in any way.

But first I want to talk about earth energy.

Earth energy encompasses natural foods and natural medicine.

Empaths are usually very drawn to Earth energy in this stage. Why? Because Earth energy is a very different energy. It charges your body in a very different way than anything else.

- Earth energy is very powerful yet grounding.

- Instead of a domino effect, it affects both bodies at the same time. It's about as close as you will ever get to dealing with balanced energy.

- Earth energy energizes the bodies in an entirely different manner; as opposed to circling and saturating, it feeds directly into your system.

When we're talking about negativity, low vibrational frequencies, and live energy, these things surround the body, which you begin to soak up like a sponge, as it saturates the energetic body. It then becomes part of your spiritual body's foundation. Earth energy feeds directly into your system, which is different.

Next let's talk about Universal Energy. You as an Empath have a very special connection with Universal energy. When your energy awareness is heightened, you quickly become very "in tune" with the ebb and flow of Universal energy.

This is my favorite. I love working with Universal energy. And when I learned how to tune into Universal energy, I was blown away by how it works with your Empath abilities.

There are two things you have in common with other Empaths. These very important things you should know are:

1) Empaths are powerful manifestors.

I mean, powerful beyond belief. Your spiritual body is built and wired to work with Universal energy. You are built to work with the Law of Attraction. You could not be more naturally set up to gain some super amazing desires in your life, to really change things for yourself, to have an entirely different lifestyle if that's what you choose.

When I started becoming healthier as an Empath, I was so grateful to have this connection. My lifestyle entirely changed.

I began working from home, and I created multiple six-figure incomes. Not having to answer to anyone, working on my own time, finding my passion teaching, and doing something that I thoroughly enjoyed, all while being able to watch my grandbabies if I needed to or go to lunch that day if I wanted. It was the most amazing, fulfilling feeling ever. And you are no different from me. **You are a very powerful manifestor...**

2) Empaths are also moon children.

Which means as an Empath, you have a very special connection with Universal energy. And when your energetic awareness is heightened, you quickly tune in to the ebb and flow of Universal energy. As an Empath, you have such an edge over everybody else.

In the Spiritual Awareness stage, you learn how to develop a stronger relationship with energy. This is also when you begin to develop your energetic dictionary.

An *energetic dictionary* is very important because it helps your physical brain make sense of what your spiritual body is experiencing. And you develop this skill by learning:

- How to differentiate between *different types* of Empath energy.

- How good energy feels, and how toxic energy feels.

- How the physical body is affected.

What's the most powerful thing that happens when you start developing your energetic dictionary?

You begin training your spiritual and physical bodies on how to work together as a team, instead of separately.

This is when you begin your very first stages of Empath development. And it feels good...I learned so much:

~ I learned how to manage my ability better.

~ I learned about energetic saturation.

~ I learned what things I was holding on to without realizing I was holding on to them. (Before learning about energetic hoarding, I just thought it was the emotional space I was in at the time.)

~ I learned that I needed to compartmentalize and understand how these things were really affecting my health.

~ I learned very quickly that I needed to make changes regarding how this energy I was subjecting myself to was affecting my health.

~ I learned how to let go...let go of all the energetic junk I thought was just part of life.

But quickly I realized this system I had been working with for so long was not just part of life, it was how I was taught. **Society teaches and promotes discord and labels it normal.** And I wanted no part of that kind of normal anymore!

Then I learned about maintenance, and how to be more aware of how to live in a physical world with a very spiritual, powerful body.

So I retrained myself on how to do things and how to exist with other people who are not Empaths. Also how to exist with the physical energy that surrounds me. And it was so awesome!

Which brings us to our next building block stage five: Spiritual Sponge.

CHAPTER 18
Stage 5 - Spiritual Sponge

By the time you've hit this stage in your Empath awakening you will have started making some progress...

By developing a stronger relationship with energy.

- Learning how to recognize energy and familiarize yourself with how it feels.

- Learning to differentiate the difference between how good energy feels and how toxic energy feels.

- Learning how to practice and experiment with those energies by embracing some and keeping others at bay.

- Understanding how you are wired and built differently than other *regular or normal* people, and what that means.

By developing your energetic dictionary.

- Learning about the five different types of energy and how some are easier to read than others.

- Learning how to differentiate *between the different types of Empath energy.*

- Learning how to work with the energy you encounter and surround yourself with instead of against it.

- Learning how to recognize when you're hoarding energy (stopping the flow of energy).

- Learning how to release energy (encouraging the flow of energy).

By training your spiritual and physical bodies how to work together as a team.

- Learning how to recognize when you're not in balance and when you are in balance.

- Learning how important it is to keep your spiritual and physical bodies working together as a team. (It's imperative. Especially, when you are learning how to become a powerful Empath.)

The Spiritual Sponge stage is where you will build upon this process. Giving your brain more important information on how to help it compartmentalize and tie everything together.

Your brain craves knowledge.

During this Empath stage, you will begin the art of "fine-tuning" your Empath ability. And when your bodies start working together, the brain wants to help, but it cannot help in the manner it's craving, unless it has the knowledge to do so.

Your physical and spiritual bodies are designed to work together; they want to work together. But we can easily drive a wedge between them and this process by ignoring one of the bodies or the other, creating discord or imbalance.

Ignoring your physical body as you develop on a spiritual level is not helpful, the same as ignoring the spiritual body most of your life while you focusing upon your physical existence is also not helpful. They really want to work together; they naturally want to work as a team. And your brain wants to help, not hinder. But to do that it needs knowledge, direction, and guidance.

This is when you want to:

- Narrow down where your gifts are useful and helpful.

- Narrow down where your focus should be.

But it's not always easy. Since you are just learning how to navigate this area, this is the stage where most people get ***stuck in an informational traffic jam or find themselves having spiritual roadblocks.***

Informational traffic jams and spiritual roadblocks happen to a lot of people. Whether you're trying to work with your Empath abilities or trying to work with any of your other psychic senses, this can be a pretty common problem. There are usually three main reasons spiritual roadblocks tend to happen during this stage:

1) You are following the crowd.

2) You are trying to practice everything at once.

3) You don't have a system to sort through the abundance of information.

When you can avoid these blocks, this is another really cool stage because it's where you will begin to blossom as an Empath. And I want you to blossom, so let's deconstruct the blocks...

Block #1 - Problems with following the crowd.

People develop spiritual roadblocks when they follow the crowd. I've had a lot of clients who have come to me and said, *I can't develop any further than I am. I'm doing everything!* (And they really are doing everything.)

So, I ask, *where'd you learn this?* The simple answer is they are following the crowd. And the crowd says you must practice everything at the same time, pretty much every day. This is false information.

The thing with a spiritual sponge stage is everybody's different. And this stage is when individuality becomes more apparent. A lot of times people assume that everyone else who's on a spiritual journey knows where they're going, and most of the time they don't. Not to mention it's called a journey for a reason.

But even if they did, that doesn't work anyway because:

- You have a different purpose than everyone else.

- You have different abilities or combination of abilities than everyone else.

- You have different desires than everyone else.

Discovering your individuality is a good thing, however this can definitely cause confusion when searching for information and eventually spiritual roadblocks.

It's an important step when you learn that you're not just different from other people who are not Empaths, but you are also different from other Empaths.

The things you need to grow, develop, and blossom will be different for you than it is for ALL other people.

So it's important to have a goal in mind. Not just discovering what you need to do to be a healthy Empath, but what you need to do as a unique Empath. This can be fine-tuned with a system.

Following what everyone else is doing can lead to some pretty hefty roadblocks. For instance, when you know someone else who's on a spiritual journey and they seem to be having good results, it's natural to think, *I like their results, so I'm going to follow that route and do the things they're doing.*

However, often those who you choose to follow are just winging it. They are learning what works and what doesn't as they go, and whether they're winging it or not, your purpose is going to be different than that person. So you are going to have to navigate your own journey differently.

Even knowing this you might still be thinking, *But I need to go this way because I feel like I'm failing, and they are having success.*

If you feel like you're failing, this can make things worse, because when you follow someone else's path, it typically results in you ignoring your own intuition.

And when you veer away from your intuition, life starts to feel hard, and a spiritual journey feels like too much work.

As you learn how to develop your spiritual self by working with your Empath abilities, and learning how to navigate your intuitive senses, any spiritual fog (that haze you've most likely been experiencing) will begin to lift and clear. When that happens, it allows you to see where your path is as opposed to following somebody else's path. And that's really important.

But it comes in steps.

1) Learning about what an Empath ability really means is first.

2) Then learning about the different types of energy and what energies appear stronger to you at the moment.

3) Then learning how to hone in that specific area and really create a relationship with energy.

4) Then creating an energetic dictionary as you start really understanding how the energy eco system works.

During this part of your awakening is when the fog will begin to lift, your spiritual compass will become clearer, and you'll be able to start seeing the road in front of you.

Block #2 - Problems with practicing everything at once.

As you've probably discovered there's a lot of information out there to navigate...

When you crave knowledge, you want to learn as much as you possibly can. You start exploring. You want to learn everything to soak it all in.

You're going to find there's a lot of information to navigate and a lot of contradictory information out there. This is a huge problem in the metaphysical and spiritual industry. Lots of contradictory information.

There are so many different techniques for everything, it's mind-boggling, and teachers all teach differently.

- The amount of different information out there is endless.

- There are many different techniques for everything.

- Teachers all teach differently.

- Belief systems on how you accomplish these things or how you develop your gifts on a spiritual journey are also very different depending upon the person.

So instead of feeling informed, it can leave you feeling overwhelmed, and when you try to put it all together, it can feel like energetic chaos.

What happens when you try to practice everything you learn at once? You don't move forward; you spin in circles.

I would say this is one of the most common problems for those trying to educate themselves further. You feel like, *I've got to meditate for 15 minutes a day, I have to ground myself, oh and there's clearing stuff, and I want to eliminate negativity, I definitely need to be doing that.*

The next thing you know, you're doing 15 different things, and feeling like you're going nowhere. New clients often come to me confused, feeling stuck. So this will be the first thing I address: what's your system, and how are you working on your development?

They say things like:

- I'm doing this meditation in the morning and that meditation at night.

- I clear everything before a meditation and set intentions.

- I do a prayer before trying to connect with my guides and make sure I have my crystals.

- I need to ground myself before and after (spiritual or social event).

- I can't forget to practice (spiritual tools) for 30 minutes three times a week.

- Before I practice my spiritual tools, I do a clearing and a prayer, sit with intention, connect with white light energy.

- All while going to work, taking care of kids/family, and keeping the household in order.

Meanwhile, they are all working with different belief systems, different teachers, and doing too many different things, just spinning their wheels. Tuning into the spirit realm and your abilities does not need to be so hard. That's not a thing. That's a mindset.

A mindset formed by the information you've read, the teachers who have taught you, and your own belief system.

Here's something you might find interesting. **For those who naturally connect with their spiritual senses, this process will feel very normal and easy.**

So easy in fact, that those same people do not think they are doing anything even when they are connecting.

They think when they connect with source energy, the feeling should be powerful and noticeably different.

You might think, *I'm not doing it right because I've read (or have been taught) it feels like (stronger, powerful, different). And I'm not getting that feeling or sensation.* While that is true for those who have not been tuned into the spirit realm their whole life, it might not be the case for you. You might be one who's had a natural connection since you were young. And if you are one of these people this connection will feel **normal, anticlimactic even.**

However, you might not know that, so you overcomplicate the process, chasing this grand feeling that solidifies your connection when there's a much simpler process.

Block #3 - There needs to be a simple system.

Using all the spiritual information that you've learned thus far and mixing all these techniques together would be like trying to make a dessert from scratch with no recipe. Here's what it would look like in spiritual terms.

- *Taking ingredients from a German chocolate cake, carrot cake, and banana cream pie, then mixing it all together* = Taking these techniques from people, the internet, different teachers, and practicing them all at once.

- *Throwing the dessert into the oven to bake in the same pan for a specific amount of time* = Taking these systems and techniques, blending them together with no separation or clear focus, while anticipating wonderful results.

- *Then taking it out of the oven, tasting it, and wondering what the heck happened!* = Wondering what's going on when you are stuck, or not seeing the results you are looking for.

It's very common for students and even teachers in the spiritual field to overcomplicate the process. First, the proper information and explanations are often times missing. *Why do you need to do this? Why do you need to do it that way? What's the purpose?*

Secondly, there are too many techniques that are overcomplicated. You can almost always cut your process and the things they require in half or more, because it's really all about the basics.

Adding more stuff doesn't make anything go faster, or better, especially in the spiritual world. You've just added a bunch of unnecessary steps.

Proper techniques and simplicity are the secret ingredient. But even with a secret ingredient, you need a system...

That's why I've created the SPIRIT System

It's so important to have a system when you are experiencing an Empath awakening. A system that teaches you how to filter through all the junk you don't need.

Otherwise, you can spend a lot of time spinning your wheels, feeling like you are not advancing or accomplishing anything. And it can be frustrating...

There's a simple system I've developed for you to follow. My SPIRIT system is an easy-to-follow navigation technique you can use when you're in this Empath awakening stage.

1) Seek, Explore, & Experiment: Try different things, test the waters, *explore everything.*

Maybe you feel strong working with people energy, but you may want to test the waters with some of your other psychic senses. Maybe you want to explore and experiment with claircognizance or clairvoyance and see which gift you feel the most drawn to or feel the most excited about. Try it! Try it all out; something is going to feel really good. When that happens, head down that road.

2) Process of Elimination: Concentrate on the areas you are the most drawn to first. *Pick one to start with.* Once you become familiar with that one, then you can add something else.

This is a really good time, giving yourself permission to just focus upon the areas you are the most drawn to. Instead of doing too many things at once, get really good at one thing first. Then add more into the mix. When you get really good at something and add another thing into the mix, it's called layering. It's such a good part of the process.

3) Invest and Commit: Once you pick an area, *investing the time and committing* to your awakening/craft is important.

This will be what sets you apart from other people. It will be what sets your development rate apart from other people. How quickly you feel strong and empowered. This applies to most things even if you are changing your diet or starting a new exercise routine. If you invest your time and commit to something, you will usually accomplish something you feel really good about.

4) Rid Yourself of Useless Information: As you are gathering information and *learning to let go of any information that doesn't serve or resonate with you is important.* If you don't like it, release it.

When I was a young Empath, I was taught a lot of useless information that definitely didn't help me in my everyday life. As you can probably tell, I'm all about simplicity because everything's overcomplicated, especially when it comes to spiritual information. I wanted things that helped enhance my life on a day-to-day basis. So keep the information that resonates with you, and let go of the rest.

5) Invent Your Own Technique: It's important to *create your own unique technique and system.* One that works specifically for you, with your abilities. Take bits and pieces of the techniques that resonate with you from everywhere and create your own technique.

I got rid of a lot of the useless information for you in this book. However, that doesn't mean you're still going to resonate with all the systems that I'm putting in place for you. I do highly recommend that you go through them until you are very familiar with creating your own system, though. Then invent your own techniques, ones that work specifically for you, with your unique abilities. You might be wondering, *How do I do that?* By taking bits and pieces of techniques that resonate with you from everywhere and creating your own technique.

I use a lot of the techniques I've been talking about throughout this book, but I don't always use them every day. I use some daily, others once a week, and some just as needed—because I create my own techniques.

6) Training: Once you've narrowed down where to focus, and you begin developing your own technique, training is important. If you are serious, it can include classes or finding a mentor.

By the time you've worked through the Spiritual Sponge stage, things will really start to flow more fluidly. You've put in some good work:

- Building a solid foundation.

- Learning how to synchronize your bodies.

- Putting some good systems in place.

- Working on fine-tuning your Empath abilities.

Now it's time to release anything that's holding you back from propelling forward. This is when you flow right into stage six... Spiritual Release!

CHAPTER 19
Stage 6 – Spiritual Release

This stage is what I call the honeymoon phase because it feels wonderful. Once you've put in the work, such as:

- Proper training or finding a mentor.

- You're working with a system.

- Put the time and/or money into understanding how to move forward.

This is when things really start to "click" and work out for you. It's also the stage when you begin to work with the law of allowing.

You start relaxing and stop resisting. You learn how to work more fluidly with the Universal Laws, such as the Law of Allowing.

The Law of Allowing enables things to move without resistance and to evolve and grow naturally.

This is one of my favorite laws, and I think one of the most important Universal Laws. Most people really struggle with this one because of conditioning. We've been trained to think differently for most of our lives.

When you naturally begin working with the Law of Allowing, you also begin the process of retraining your brain. And it's awesome!

I'm sure you've heard about the Law of Attraction, but working with the Law of Attraction doesn't work very well until you've learned how to work with the Law of Allowing. *To attract, you have to allow; one doesn't work without the other.*

You learn so much resistance growing up. Resistance to anything you're fearful of, or your parents, family, and friends are fearful of. Resistance to your gifts because they make no sense or there's no proof. There's so much resistance built up in everybody by the time you're in your late teens or early twenties, you're just bracing yourself for the worst-case scenario when it comes to life in general.

Waiting for the next bad thing to happen, worrying about your future, or the unknown, and just being fearful things won't work out the way you hope they will. This is why the Law of Allowing is such an important Universal Law.

The Law of Allowing dictates that all Universal Energy runs in currents, and these currents have a flow.

- When you allow the Universal flow to evolve and grow naturally, things will begin to manifest in a fluid, non-chaotic manner.

- You are allowing the Universe to create and manifest freely with no interference.

- This law feels the most *unnatural* to most people because our brain is not "trained" to allow. We've been trained to think that *allowing is being lazy.*

- **The state of allowing is the purest state of manifesting.**

Most people really struggle with this concept because of the conditioning they've received most of their life. When you begin working with the Law of Allowing, you also begin the process of retraining your brain to allow space for spiritual, energetic, and universal law knowledge. It's the most amazing, freeing feeling. This knowledge is powerful! And you can feel it to the core of your soul...

You still must take action when working with these laws, however, allowing is more about ***not trying to control the outcome after you've taken action.*** It's about allowing something to unfold after you've put in the work and trying not to micro-manage the outcome. Such as thinking:

This is not right.
I see it in my head this way.
It needs to be like xyz.
This is not how I envisioned it.

You need to be open, open to other paths and other outcomes that *allow the same feeling to unfold as an end result.* When you are in a state of mind that has one outcome, or you're micro-managing your desired outcome, you limit yourself.

You limit yourself because when you're dealing with Universal energy, the universe has more abundance and flow to it than your brain can envision. By trying to control an outcome, you're really limiting the universe, its energy, and its energetic flow. You are handcuffing the energy you want to work with. As an Empath, this is the last thing you want to do, especially because...

Empaths are very powerful manifesters, as they have been gifted a unique ability to work with energy and a unique understanding about energy that other people don't have.

By this stage you should have:

- A better understanding of energy.

- A better relationship with energy.

- A better understanding of the relationship between your thoughts and energy, and how that process works.

With this understanding comes knowledge about how everything works universally and energetically, and this knowledge can bring about a lot of change in your life.

This stage is when you will finally feel like you are gaining some traction and more control.

If you choose to use your natural Empath ability to help you become a powerful manifester, you will begin to view things a bit differently. Your understanding of how the world works will shift. You will start feeling or thinking things like:

Oh, that's how it works.
Okay, this feels good to me.
I need to put more of this energy out there.

This is also when the torch passes from the physical body to the spiritual and the spiritual body becomes a lot more powerful.

- You'll naturally begin to tune into your spiritual body more often. You won't be fighting it and resisting so much.

- You will be way more trusting when it comes to letting your spiritual body take a more active role and allowing your spiritual senses guide you.

- You begin to trust signs, signals, and information you receive from the spiritual realm.

You will work more with the Law of Allowing and work with Universal Energy better, which allows you to release old patterns that no longer serve you. This is huge for Empaths who like to hoard energy.

This stage also encompasses three very important things...

Releasing, Trusting, and Allowing.

1) Releasing old thoughts and thought patterns. When you are ready to do this, it could not feel better, it's so freeing! There's usually a light bulb moment, where all the information "clicks," and you'll have some great realizations:

Oh, that's why this stuff wasn't working for me.

I get it now, because this is how the world/energy/universe actually works.

I can finally see how I was causing myself blocks.

Releasing old thought patterns and embracing new knowledge can bring a lot of clarity and aha moments. It feels so good to have this clarity, you will no longer desire to hold on to old beliefs. You will no longer feel the desire to hold on to old energetic junk to fix it; you just want to let it go...

You are not just letting go of old thought patterns and ideas, but the energy that encompasses those thoughts and ideas.

All thoughts and beliefs hold an energetic vibration, and that vibration will weave its way deeply into your energetic system and become part of your spiritual body.

That is where energetic hoarding happens, in the deepest part of your emotional body and your energetic system.

Empaths tend to gather up emotional energy from other people. When you gather their energy and hold onto other people's stuff, you make it part of your stuff. Naturally, as an Empath, you feel you can iron this energy out for them, heal the discord, and somehow, it'll trickle back into their life.

But that's not what happens. It will energetically trickle its way into your life, adjusting your own frequency to theirs, and weaving its way deep down into your system.

The good news is you can also rid yourself of these energetic webs and learn how to release them. And when you do, it becomes very noticeable.

You feel lighter! *Energetically and spiritually lighter...*

The more you tune into and become aware of your spiritual body, the more aware you become of spiritual energy as a whole. This awareness of spiritual energy helps you develop a very trusting relationship with your spiritual body.

2) Trusting your spiritual body and your spiritual senses. As your spiritual body becomes more powerful, *spiritual energy will feel stronger.* As a result, your connection to the spiritual realm becomes a lot more noticeable.

This allows you to gain more clarity and have more confidence when receiving information from the spiritual realm because the energy behind it is more noticeable. Even if you don't have physical proof, there's a strength behind it that you really can't ignore. Whether it be from spirit guides, angels, or just spiritual realm information, your comfort level begins to rise.

The combination of learning how to release old thought patterns and energetic junk, and trusting your spiritual body, amplifies your awareness of Universal Energy. This is important when learning how to allow the flow of Universal energy.

3) Allowing the flow of Universal Energy. Universal Energy is always meant to be flowing like a river, and when you learn how to tune into it, *you can feel when it's not flowing properly.*

If you find that a river is pooling up somewhere, cluttered with debris, you can see that it's not flowing properly. It's the same thing with energy, only instead of seeing it, you can feel when clutter or energetic debris is hindering the flow of energy. Instead of sticks and debris, energetic clutter is caused by resistance.

To allow you must master one very simple technique. *If you don't resist flow, you allow flow.*

For instance, if you're feeling resistance against a certain outcome, or you're feeling worried or fearful, energy will begin knotting up, hindering energetic flow, and it can cause a lot of issues.

When you hoard emotional energy that doesn't belong to you, energy of family members or different people in your life that makes you uncomfortable, when you pull that frequency into your energetic field, if you don't release it, it sticks there. What you end up with is energetic clutter and debris in your own energetic field that really doesn't belong to you. This will hinder your flow; stagnant energy will pool, which prevents fresh, clean, and free-flowing energy from moving about your system. And you don't want to do that.

You want to allow flow.

Part of the trust factor with the Law of Allowing stems from the belief that there's only a limited number of things in the world and all good things are already taken, or untouchable by you. Universal Law dictates this is not true on both accounts.

Trust in the flow and the creative power of the Universe, of something bigger than you.

Trust in the notion that you deserve happiness in everything you do, relationships and otherwise.

Then allow the flow of Universal Energy... It's very powerful!

Which brings us to stage seven... Spiritual Clearing!

NOTE: If you'd like to learn more about Universal Laws, I've written a whole book on this you might enjoy. You can find that here: *Universal Laws: 18 Powerful Laws & The Secrets Behind Manifesting Your Desires.*

CHAPTER 20

Stage 7 – Spiritual Clearing & Development

Once you've worked through the release stage, you will definitely feel the urge to declutter and reorganize your life. You will feel the need to clear your energetic house.

There are 3 main areas of your energetic house.

1) Your spiritual house – This includes your spiritual and emotional bodies, spiritual energy, and universal energy.

2) Your relationship house – This includes your emotional body, and who you exchange energy with, or people energy and earth energy.

3) Your physical house – This includes your physical body, places, items or things which you surround yourself with, and physical energy.

You're past the awareness stage, and by this stage your spiritual body is becoming more powerful. *This makes you very hypersensitive to what's going on in your energetic house.*

Clearing Your Spiritual House

Your spiritual house will include your spiritual body and your emotional body as well as your thoughts, beliefs, and perspectives.

During the spiritual clearing stage, you feel the urge to take charge of your life and have a stronger desire to consciously make different choices.

This is the stage where you'll start restructuring your belief system and creating a new belief system. You'll be retraining your brain to see things differently. You'll become a lot more aware of what thoughts are coming in and going out because you realize they have a ***major impact*** on your physical and spiritual environment.

- When you have a better understanding of how much these things directly affect your life experience, it prompts you to want to make different decisions based on a spiritual point of view instead of a physical point of view. From a place of understanding the connection between energy, thoughts, and outcome.

- When you learn how to work with energy and understand how energy is dictated by your thoughts to create an outcome, you'll come to realize when you have a perspective that doesn't feel good or has a lower vibration or a negative undertone to it. Energetically, if you don't release it, you will be projecting a lower vibrational outcome.

This entails monitoring yourself so you can create new habits and patterns.

When a perspective doesn't feel good, because you're irritated, angry, or edgy, you need to release it.

*If a belief doesn't feel good,
you need to release it.*

*If a thought doesn't feel good,
you need to release it.*

Release any perspective, belief, or thought that no longer feels good to you. This includes fear and worry.

Yet people almost always do the opposite.

They hoard those emotions and obsess over them, which is exactly the opposite of anything you would want to do because all that does is **keep a low vibrational frequency active within your system.** It's like throwing lighter fluid on a fire (obsessing over an emotion or feeling) to keep it burning as long as you can until you run out of lighter fluid (until you get distracted with another emotion or feeling).

This is why it's so important to train yourself how not to do this; you don't want to be the one responsible for keeping low vibrational frequencies active in your own system. But if you do this, you are ultimately responsible. No one else can be responsible no matter how you try to twist it around. They are your emotions that belong to you and your emotional response to anything is dictated by you.

But you're not going to be able to do this overnight. It takes time...

Let's say you've had ten negative thoughts today that had a negative undertone to them. If you can get that down to seven tomorrow, or even the next day, this is progress. Even your awareness and your conscientious thought process on trying to shift those thoughts is going to be huge.

But it's going to take some work. Just think of all the years you've lived creating your thought pattern and habits. You've lived your whole life up until this point creating and building your current belief system.

This is not something that happened quickly. You've built it, you've created it, you're used to it. Your perspective and belief system are built upon this foundation.

Clearing Your Relationship House

Your relationship house will include anyone who you have an energetic exchange with. This encompasses all the people in your life.

This means releasing a lot of emotional junk tied or attached to other people, and in some instances the relationship itself. This can include:

- Unhealthy emotions tied to a relationship.

- Toxic or unhealthy relationships with other people.

The interesting thing about emotional energy is it holds weight; it can feel heavy or light. It's common for people to want to hand this weight to you. They want you to help carry their burden because they can feel the weight of their own emotions. If they find someone willing to engage with their emotional junk, an energetic exchange takes place.

As an Empath and healer, it's a natural urge to not only allow this to happen, but even encourage it. When you feel energetic discord, even with another person, naturally you want to try to help them fix it. When you do this, people will naturally gravitate towards you.

They will want to pile their emotional junk on top of you. When people push their emotional stuff (energy) onto another person, they temporarily feel better. This is an energetic exchange.

This energetic weight projects outwards from their body, and when you engage, you grab onto it and pull it into your energetic field. Often, they do this not only to feel lighter, but to shift blame onto someone else. They don't have to take responsibility for feeling any type of way; they don't have to take responsibility for changing their situation or be proactive in any way to shift it.

I've now put it all on you, now it's in your area, in your house. You need to help me fix this.

This will include emotions tied to a relationship such as anger, holding a grudge, sadness, worry, stress, hurt, any low vibrational frequencies. This is the stuff you want to clear out of your relationship house. You want to clear out all the junk, toxic and unhealthy relationships with other people. It's not just emotional junk, it's heavily weighted energy, which means it can weigh you down energetically.

If you're with somebody who makes you feel uplifted and positive who you're having fun with, you don't want to clear that out of your relationship house.

Paying very close attention to who you surround yourself with is very important during this stage. When you're clearing your relationship house, you want to pay close attention to how the relationships in your life make you feel.

Do they make you feel good or not so good?

Are the people needy?

Are they inspiring?

What is their impact on your life?

How do you feel when you are around them?

Happy, stressed, worried, or hopeful?

How do you feel after being around them? Good, tired, drained, or energized?

I have an exercise to break this down visually. When you are dealing with energy, it's good to make things as visual as you can. This helps your brain make sense of something it can't see.

- Take a piece of paper and make three columns. Label them Good, Not So Good, and Awareness.

- Next make a list of everybody you surround yourself with.

- Anybody who makes you feel better, put in the Good category.

- Anybody who makes you feel not so great, put them in the Not So Good category.

- For those who can go either way, put them in the Awareness category. That category you're going to want to pay some particular attention to.

- Simply categorizing your relationship house can give you a visual of your energetic environment because of the huge role relationships play.

You should find this exercise helpful because you will start noticing what kind of effect and impact your people are having on your life.

The more you pay attention to your relationship house, you will notice how relationships affect your current life experience. It's not just while you are together; there are usually after-effects that spill over into more of your day than you might realize. These after-effects can also shift the energetic flow you're creating for yourself. This is why it's so important to learn how to monitor the vibration of your relationship house. *People tend to hoard stuff in their relationship house the most.*

They like to keep this house full of energy. Good energy or bad, any energy feels better than less energy when it comes to their relationship house for most people. What you might not know is...

Your relationship house holds and maintains an energetic vibration. This vibration is dictated by the sum of all the energy placed and held there.

Low vibration - If the vibration you hold there is on the lower end, it constricts your relationship house, and high-vibration relationships will be pushed out or blocked from coming in. *All vibrations attract other like vibrations.*

High vibration – If the vibration you hold in this house is on the higher end, it will expand and grow, making room for more high vibration energy. *It can also minimize the impact of lower vibrations sneaking through.*

When making your list, if you have more people in the Awareness category than you have in the Good category, that combination is going to dictate the energetic vibration for you in your relationship house.

This is why low vibrational people (Not So Good category) will be one of the things you want to be very aware of. If you notice you have more people on that side of your list, you'll need to check the energetic vibration of your house. Most likely you have created a low-vibration environment here, which means you are going to have to monitor your relationship house better.

This is going to require that you release low-vibration conductors, any junk that's not feeling good to you. You may have to minimize the time you spend with people on the low-vibration side, as it will affect your own vibration. When you are working hard to keep your vibration on the higher side, low vibrations can act like virus.

If the vibration you hold in your relationship house is on the higher side, it will expand and grow, making room for more high-vibrational energy. It can also minimize the impact of lower vibrations trying to sneak through, which they will. And that's really awesome.

If you take charge of your relationship house ***and really pay attention to what the sum is of all the energy you are holding there,*** it can make such a huge impact in your life.

Clearing Your Physical House

Your physical house includes anything in your physical space, items you surround yourself with, and places you visit.

This is the simplest of all your energetic houses. Because you are dealing with physical spaces and things. You will want to make sure you:

1) Declutter and organize physical spaces. – Chaotic spaces create a chaotic energy flow.

2) Dust and clean physical items. Dust and dirt will hold residual energy, usually energy you will want to get rid of.

3) Rid yourself of any unused or unwanted items. Unwanted and unused items also hold residual energy that usually doesn't serve you well.

4) Be very conscientious of the places you visit. Places can all hold residual energy, or energy imprints. It's good to steer clear of places of low-vibration energy.

You want to make sure that you declutter and organize physical spaces. Chaotic spaces create chaotic energy streams and entanglements, which can result in stuck energy. Dirt and dust will hold residual energy, and this is the energy you will want to get rid of. You don't want to keep this energy; you want to release it and allow it to move on.

Paying a lot of attention to your physical space is important for an Empath.

How free flowing is it?

What vibration does it hold?

A higher vibration or a lower vibration?

Any energy that's stuck or blocked is energetic debris. We want to keep that energetic river flowing, bringing in new energy to replace old energy, fresh and clean energy, because the cleaner you keep that energy, the stronger the flow. Clean, strong energy will bring new things and new energy into your life.

- Replace broken items
- Get rid of excess
- Clear out clutter
- Clean items that are dingy or need dusting
- Organize and compartmentalize things

Spiritual Clearing Leads to Development...

Once you've worked on clearing your energetic houses, nothing is standing in your way, so many times it leads to some major advancements. Such as heightened ability with:

- Dream communication
- Spirit communication
- Spirit guide communication
- Angel communication
- Other gifts or "clairs" develop quickly or out of nowhere

At this stage of the game, you have been creating a solid relationship with your spiritual body, and your belief system is different. You have a much more cohesive relationship between the spiritual world and the physical world. And all things start to make sense in a very different manner.

How your spiritual body operates with things you can't see, and how you can bring that into your physical life with things that you can see. You can make more sense of how everything works together as a whole, instead of separately. And with this knowledge comes a lot more clarity, and it raises your vibrational frequency in a very powerful way.

You are on the road to becoming an Empowered Empath!

Working through and mastering these stages will greatly enhance your day-to-day life; things will shift and change.

- You will feel happier or more "whole."

- Opportunities seem to surface more often.

- Different things you were struggling with before seem to be resolving quicker and more naturally.

You are now working with all the gifts you were born with; you are working with spiritual energy, physical energy, and Universal energy as a whole unit instead of separately. This is when you start becoming more empowered.

Everything should be flowing better. You've learned how to stop your resistance, you've learned what resistance does to you energetically, and you've learned how that translates into your life experience and into the physical realm.

CHAPTER 21

Bridging the Gap

I've covered a lot of information in this book—I know it's a lot to consume—but there's more...
You need to change many things in your life when you discover that you have an Empath ability, especially if you are struggling and trying to wrestle it into working properly. And this change is going to require steps.

Education and a mindset adjustment:

- Educating your self better with knowledge that encompasses the spiritual realm, spiritual body, and how you truly function when operating from a place of **wholeness.**

- Not only enhancing your knowledge as far as the spiritual aspect goes but also enhancing your knowledge on the physical realm as well.

- Learning about limitations in the physical realm,

and how the physical realm is meant to heavily include spiritual aspects.

- Understanding how most people live their day to day based upon a failed system, one that doesn't embrace wholeness and wellness.

Breaking bad habits and patterns:

- Learning how most people have been trained to become physically based thinkers.

- Learning how you've been taught to throw out spiritual information and connections and compartmentalizing them as invalid.

- Learning how most people have lived their life physically dominant which will lead to imbalance and spiritual discord.

- Learning how most people have structured their entire existence based upon this flawed premise.

Disruption and change:

- It's time to change your ideals and beliefs when it comes to health, wellness, and your spiritual body.

- It's time to restructure your life in a way that encompasses wholeness and balance between the physical and spiritual realms.

- It's time to learn how to empower and strengthen your energetic body.

And this is where the next part of your Empath journey begins. Learning how to achieve proper balance by empowering and strengthening your energy, your body, your mind.

It's going to take some time, and it's going to take shifting your lifestyle and the way you are currently doing things. You are going to learn more about your weaknesses and how to counterbalance those weaknesses with strength. It's going to be informative, it's going to be eye opening, and it's going to be the best gift you've ever given yourself...

If you're ready to take the next step of this powerful journey, it's time to move on to book 2.

Empowered Empath: The Ultimate Guide to Learning How to Achieve Balance & Wellness by Empowering & Strengthening Your Energy.

Scan to download my FREE

Quantum Heart Activation Meditation™

https://quantumheart.net/quantum-heart-meditation

About the Author

Aloha Beautiful Soul!

My name is Jennifer O'Neill. I am the founder of **Empath University™** and **Quantum Heart™**, a body of work devoted to awakening the multidimensional intelligence of the heart.

I've always been able to feel energy moving through people, places, and timelines for as long as I can remember. This awareness has shaped the way I understand healing, consciousness, and the intelligence that moves through all things.

My earliest memories include sensing and working with the Quantum Heart Field, long before I had language for what I was experiencing.

Today, I teach others how to access this field as a gateway to healing, coherence, and expanded consciousness. Through my books, classes, and quantum activations, I guide people on how to release inherited patterns, dissolve outdated timelines, and align with their highest quantum reality.

My work bridges the seen and unseen. Combining spiritual insight with energetic awareness to support emotional healing, spiritual awakening, and conscious evolution.

The heart isn't just where love lives. It's where your universe begins.

— Jennifer O'Neill

Channel • Medical Medium • Spiritual Teacher • International Speaker & Author

Quantum Heart Website: https://quantumheart.net/

Empath University: http://empath-university.com

- amazon.com/stores/Jennifer-ONeill/author/B007C6LDRY
- substack.com/@thequantumuniverse
- youtube.com/@JenniferOneillHealer
- pinterest.com/thequantumuniverse
- instagram.com/thequantum_universe
- facebook.com/JenniferONeillAuthor
- tiktok.com/@thequantumheart?
- linkedin.com/in/jennifer-o-neill-20b32821
- x.com/keystothespirit

www.ingramcontent.com/pod-product-compliance
Lightning Source LLC
LaVergne TN
LVHW040116080426
835507LV00039B/384